FAVORITE BRAND NAME™

Made | Simple™

Chicken

Publications International, Ltd.

Favorite Brand Name Recipes at www.fbnr.com

Photography on pages 7, 17, 37, 39, 51, 55, 57, 63, 65, 105, 111, 113, 129, 143, 147, 149 and 151 by Stephen Hamilton Photographics, Chicago.

Photographers: Tate Hunt, Jennifer Marx
Photographers' Assistant: Lindsay Fair
Prop Stylist: Thomas Hamilton
Food Stylists: Donna Coates, Kim Hartman
Assistant Food Stylist: Breana Moeller

Pictured on the front cover: Pantry Fruited Chicken *(page 102).*
Pictured on the back cover: Ginger Plum Chicken *(page 74).*

ISBN-13: 978-1-4127-2572-9
ISBN-10: 1-4127-2572-0

Library of Congress Control Number: 2007920129

Manufactured in China.

8 7 6 5 4 3 2 1

Microwave Cooking: Microwave ovens vary in wattage. Use the cooking times as guidelines and check for doneness before adding more time.

Preparation/Cooking Times: Preparation times are based on the approximate amount of time required to assemble the recipe before cooking, baking, chilling or serving. These times include preparation steps such as measuring, chopping and mixing. The fact that some preparations and cooking can be done simultaneously is taken into account. Preparation of optional ingredients and serving suggestions is not included.

seared chicken with greek salsa

Salsa

- **1 small cucumber, seeded and chopped (about 1 cup total)**
- **3 tablespoons chopped fresh mint**
- **2 tablespoons finely chopped red onion**
- **1 to 2 tablespoons lemon juice**
- **½ to ¾ teaspoon grated lemon peel**
- **⅛ teaspoon salt**
- **⅛ teaspoon red pepper flakes**
- **1 ounce crumbled feta with sun-dried tomatoes and basil**

Chicken

- **4 boneless chicken breasts (about 1 pound)**
- **¾ teaspoon dried oregano**
- **¼ teaspoon salt**
- **¼ teaspoon black pepper**
- **Nonstick cooking spray**

1. Combine all salsa ingredients except feta in medium bowl. Toss gently to blend; set aside.

2. Season both sides of chicken with oregano, salt and pepper.

3. Heat large nonstick skillet over medium-high heat until hot. Coat both sides of chicken with cooking spray. Cook 5 minutes on each side or until cooked cooked through.

4. Add feta to salsa. Toss gently; serve with chicken.

Makes 4 servings

easy
dinners

chili cranberry chicken

½ cup HEINZ® Chili Sauce
½ cup whole berry cranberry sauce
2 tablespoons orange marmalade
⅛ teaspoon ground allspice
4 to 6 skinless boneless chicken breast halves (about 1½ pounds)
2 teaspoons vegetable oil

Combine first 4 ingredients; set aside. In large skillet, slowly brown chicken on both sides in oil. Pour reserved chili sauce mixture over chicken. Simmer, uncovered, 8 to 10 minutes or until chicken is cooked and sauce is of desired consistency, turning and basting occasionally.   *Makes 4 to 6 servings and about 1 cup sauce*

belgioioso® kasseri chicken

1 cup plain low-fat yogurt
1 large clove garlic, minced
½ teaspoon dried oregano leaves
¼ teaspoon black pepper
4 boneless skinless chicken breast halves
⅓ cup grated BELGIOIOSO® Kasseri Cheese

Whisk together yogurt, garlic, oregano and pepper in medium bowl. Add chicken and turn to coat. Cover and let stand 30 minutes.

Preheat broiler. Line broiler pan with foil. Remove chicken from marinade and place smooth side down on prepared pan, reserving marinade in bowl. Broil chicken 6 minutes. Turn chicken over. Brush with reserved marinade. Sprinkle with BelGioioso Kasseri Cheese and broil about 4 minutes or until chicken is cooked through. Transfer to plates. Garnish with parsley and serve.   *Makes 4 servings*

easy chicken and mushroom stroganoff

        4 boneless, skinless chicken breast halves
        2 tablespoons butter
        2 tablespoons all-purpose flour
        1 medium red onion, chopped
        8 ounces mushrooms, quartered
    1½ cups chicken broth
        2 tablespoons prepared coarse-grain mustard
        ½ cup sour cream
        3 tablespoons chopped fresh parsley
        2 cups cooked egg noodles

In large nonstick frypan, melt butter over high heat. Place flour in pie pan; add chicken and turn to coat well. Place chicken in frypan and cook, turning about 5 minutes to brown well on both sides. Stir in onion, mushrooms and any remaining flour. Reduce heat to medium and cook, stirring, until onion is golden brown, about 5 minutes.

In small bowl, whisk together chicken broth and mustard. Pour mixture into frypan and stir. Bring to a boil; reduce heat and simmer about 5 minutes. Stir in sour cream and parsley; simmer for 2 additional minutes. Season with salt and pepper to taste.

Serve over egg noodles.   *Makes 4 servings*

Tip: To freeze, transfer stroganoff to plastic container with tight-fitting lid. Let cool, uncovered, for 20 minutes. Refrigerate, uncovered, until cold, about 30 minutes. Cover tightly and freeze until needed. To thaw, transfer from freezer to refrigerator 12 to 24 hours before needed. Reheat in large, covered frypan over medium-low heat. Bring to a simmer and cook about 5 minutes.

Favorite recipe from **National Chicken Council**

roast chicken with peppers

1 chicken (3 to 3½ pounds), cut into pieces
3 tablespoons olive oil, divided
1 tablespoon plus 1½ teaspoons chopped fresh rosemary *or* 1½ teaspoons dried rosemary
1 tablespoon fresh lemon juice
1¼ teaspoons salt, divided
¾ teaspoon freshly ground black pepper, divided
3 bell peppers (preferably 1 red, 1 yellow and 1 green)
1 medium onion

1. Preheat oven to 375°F. Place chicken in shallow roasting pan.

2. Combine 2 tablespoons oil, rosemary and lemon juice; brush over chicken. Sprinkle 1 teaspoon salt and ½ teaspoon pepper over chicken. Roast 15 minutes.

3. Cut bell peppers lengthwise into ½-inch-thick strips. Cut onion into thin wedges. Toss vegetables with remaining 1 tablespoon oil, ¼ teaspoon salt and ¼ teaspoon pepper. Spoon vegetables around chicken; roast about 40 minutes or until vegetables are tender and chicken is cooked through (180°F). Serve chicken with vegetables and pan juices.

Makes 6 servings

ranch crispy chicken

¼ cup unseasoned dry bread crumbs or cornflake crumbs
1 packet (1 ounce) HIDDEN VALLEY® The Original Ranch® Salad Dressing & Seasoning Mix
6 bone-in chicken pieces

Combine bread crumbs and salad dressing & seasoning mix in a gallon-size Glad® Zipper Storage Bag. Add chicken pieces; seal bag. Shake to coat chicken. Bake chicken on an ungreased baking pan at 375°F for 50 minutes or until no longer pink in center and juices run clear.

Makes 4 to 6 servings

pantry fruited chicken

3 pounds chicken parts
1 bottle (12 ounces) LAWRY'S® Lemon Pepper Marinade, divided
1 can (29 ounces) yams or sweet potatoes, drained
1 cup canned apple pie filling
½ cup dried cranberries

Preheat oven to 375°F. Spray broiler pan bottom with nonstick cooking spray; arrange chicken skin-side-down on pan. Pour ⅔ cup Lemon Pepper Marinade over chicken. Bake 30 minutes. Turn chicken over. Arrange yams, apple pie filling and cranberries around chicken. Pour remaining Marinade over fruit and chicken. Return pan to oven and bake 30 minutes or until chicken is thoroughly cooked. Spoon pan juices over chicken and fruit before serving.

Makes 4 to 6 servings

Meal Idea: Serve with warm crusty bread or rice pilaf.

Variation: Try with LAWRY'S® Citrus Grill Marinade for another great flavor combination!

Prep Time: 5 to 10 minutes
Cook Time: 60 minutes

garlic chicken melt

4 boneless, skinless chicken breast halves (about 1¼ pounds)
1 envelope LIPTON® RECIPE SECRETS® Savory Herb with Garlic Soup Mix
1 can (14 ounces) diced tomatoes, undrained *or* 1 large tomato, chopped
1 tablespoon BERTOLLI® Olive Oil
½ cup shredded mozzarella or Monterey Jack cheese (about 2 ounces)

1. Preheat oven to 375°F. In 13×9-inch baking or roasting pan, arrange chicken. Pour soup mix blended with tomatoes and oil over chicken.

2. Bake, uncovered, 25 minutes or until chicken is thoroughly cooked.

3. Sprinkle with mozzarella cheese and bake an additional 2 minutes or until cheese is melted.

Makes 4 servings

pantry fruited chicken

catalonian stew

2 boneless skinless chicken breasts, cut into bite-size pieces

3 ounces pepperoni, diced

1 tablespoon vegetable oil

2 cans (15 ounces each) tomato sauce

3 cups chicken broth

1 cup pimiento-stuffed green olives, halved

2 tablespoons sugar

8 ounces uncooked rotini or other shaped pasta

⅓ cup chopped fresh parsley

⅛ teaspoon crushed saffron, optional

1 cup (4 ounces) SARGENTO® Fancy Mild or Sharp Cheddar Shredded Cheese

1 cup (4 ounces) SARGENTO® Fancy Monterey Jack Shredded Cheese

In Dutch oven, cook chicken and pepperoni in oil over medium heat until chicken is lightly browned, about 5 minutes; drain. Add tomato sauce, chicken broth, olives and sugar. Bring to a boil; reduce heat and simmer, covered, 15 minutes. Return to a boil. Add rotini, parsley and saffron, if desired; cover and cook an additional 15 minutes or until pasta is tender. Combine Cheddar and Monterey Jack cheeses in small bowl. Spoon stew into 6 individual ovenproof serving bowls; sprinkle evenly with cheese. Bake in preheated 350°F oven about 5 minutes or until cheese is melted. *Makes 6 servings*

chili-chicken enchiladas

Nonstick cooking spray
3 cups (12 ounces) shredded Cheddar and/or Monterey Jack cheese
1½ cups sour cream
¾ cup roasted red peppers, drained and chopped
1 can (7 ounces) ORTEGA® Diced Green Chiles
2 cups diced cooked chicken
1 can (10 ounces) ORTEGA Enchilada Sauce
8 (8-inch) ORTEGA Soft Flour Tortillas

PREHEAT oven to 350°F. Spray 13×9-inch glass baking dish with cooking spray.

RESERVE 1½ cups cheese, ½ cup sour cream and ¼ cup each red peppers and green chiles; set aside.

MIX chicken with remaining cheese, sour cream, red peppers and green chiles in medium bowl.

SPREAD about 2 teaspoons enchilada sauce over each tortilla. Top each with ½ cup chicken mixture. Roll up tortillas; arrange, seam side down, in baking dish.

TOP tortillas with remaining enchilada sauce. Sprinkle with the reserved cheese.

COVER with foil. Bake for 50 to 60 minutes or until hot, removing foil during last 5 minutes of baking time.

SPOON reserved sour cream over top and sprinkle with the reserved red peppers and green chiles.

Makes 4 servings (2 enchiladas each)

 tip | Rotisserie chicken is a great time-saver for busy cooks. Try using it for the diced cooked chicken in this recipe.

green chile-chicken casserole

4 cups shredded cooked chicken
1½ cups green enchilada sauce
1 can (10¾ ounces) condensed cream of chicken soup, undiluted
1 container (8 ounces) sour cream
1 can (4 ounces) diced mild green chiles
½ cup vegetable oil
12 (6-inch) corn tortillas
1½ cups (6 ounces) shredded Colby-Jack cheese, divided

1. Preheat oven to 325°F. Grease 13×9-inch casserole.

2. Combine chicken, enchilada sauce, soup, sour cream and chiles in large skillet. Cook and stir over medium-high heat until warm.

3. Heat oil in separate deep skillet. Fry tortillas just until soft; drain on paper towels. Place 4 tortillas on bottom of prepared casserole. Layer with one third of chicken mixture and ½ cup cheese. Repeat layers twice.

4. Bake 15 to 20 minutes or until cheese is melted and casserole is heated through.   *Makes 6 servings*

Variation: Shredded Mexican cheese blend can be substituted for Colby-Jack cheese.

 tip | For those looking for great taste and the ultimate in convenience, try new products such as precooked boneless chicken strips and chunks. These delicious products are timesavers when preparing pastas, salads, casseroles and sandwiches in a hurry.

honey lime glazed chicken

   1 broiler-fryer chicken, quartered (about 3 pounds) *or* 3 pounds chicken parts
  ⅓ cup honey
   2 tablespoons fresh lime juice
 1½ tablespoons soy sauce
   3 cups hot cooked thin noodles (3½ ounces uncooked)

1. Preheat oven to 375°F. Arrange chicken, skin side up, in single layer in shallow casserole dish or 11×7-inch baking dish.

2. Combine honey, lime juice and soy sauce in small bowl; mix well. Brush one third of honey mixture over chicken; bake 15 minutes.

3. Brush remaining honey mixture over chicken; bake 10 to 15 minutes more or until cooked through (180°F). Transfer to serving platter. Serve with noodles.

Makes 4 servings

cheesy chicken pot pie

  1 pound boneless, skinless chicken breast halves, cut into ½-inch chunks
  1 tablespoon all-purpose flour
  1 jar (1 pound) RAGÚ® Cheesy! Double Cheddar Sauce
  1 bag (16 ounces) frozen mixed vegetables, thawed
  1 prepared pastry for single-crust pie

Preheat oven to 425°F. In 2-quart casserole, toss chicken with flour. Stir in Ragú Cheesy! Sauce and vegetables. Cover casserole with prepared pastry. Press pastry around edge of casserole to seal; trim excess pastry, then flute edges. Cover with aluminum foil and bake 20 minutes. Remove foil and continue baking 20 minutes or until crust is golden and chicken is thoroughly cooked. Let stand 5 minutes before serving.

Makes 6 servings

country chicken and biscuits

1 can (10¾ ounces) condensed cream of celery soup
⅓ cup milk or water
4 boneless, skinless chicken breast halves, cooked and cut into bite-sized pieces
1 can (14½ ounces) DEL MONTE® Cut Green Beans, drained
1 can (11 ounces) refrigerated biscuits

1. Preheat oven to 375°F.

2. Combine soup and milk in large bowl. Gently stir in chicken and green beans; season with pepper, if desired. Spoon into 11×7-inch or 2-quart microwavable dish.

3. Cover with plastic wrap; slit to vent. Microwave on HIGH 8 to 10 minutes or until heated through, rotating dish once. If using conventional oven, cover with foil and bake at 375°F, 20 to 25 minutes or until hot.

4. Separate biscuit dough into individual biscuits. Immediately arrange biscuits over hot mixture. Bake in conventional oven about 15 minutes or until biscuits are golden brown and baked through.

Makes 4 servings

bbq chicken tacos

1 package ORTEGA® Taco Shells, heated
1 container (2 pounds) prepared shredded chicken in barbeque sauce, warmed
1 cup (8 ounces) prepared coleslaw
Shredded Monterey Jack cheese (optional)

FILL taco shells with chicken. Top with coleslaw and cheese, if desired.

Makes 6 servings

greek chicken

12 large cloves garlic, unpeeled
3 pounds chicken leg and thigh pieces
4 tablespoons fresh lemon juice, divided
3 tablespoons olive oil
2 tablespoons chopped fresh rosemary *or* 2 teaspoons dried rosemary
¾ teaspoon salt
½ teaspoon black pepper
1 teaspoon finely shredded lemon peel
Additional sprigs fresh rosemary and lemon slices

1. Preheat oven to 375°F. Arrange garlic in shallow roasting pan. Place chicken over garlic. Combine 2 tablespoons lemon juice, oil and rosemary in small bowl; brush evenly over chicken. Sprinkle chicken with salt and pepper. Bake 50 to 55 minutes or until cooked through (180°F). Transfer chicken to serving platter; keep warm.

2. Squeeze garlic pulp from skins; discard skins. Place garlic pulp in roasting pan; add remaining 2 tablespoons lemon juice. Cook over medium heat, mashing garlic and stirring to scrape up browned bits. Pour sauce over chicken; garnish with lemon peel and rosemary sprigs. *Makes 4 servings*

Note: Add more garlic and lemon juice to taste. Tuck a few lemon wedges or slices among the chicken pieces before roasting.

 tip | Unpeeled cloves of garlic usually burst open while roasting, making it a cinch to squeeze out the softened, creamy roasted garlic with your thumb and forefinger. If the cloves have not burst open, simply slice off the end with a knife and squeeze out the garlic.

crispy garlic chicken

1 envelope LIPTON® RECIPE SECRETS® Savory Herb with Garlic Soup Mix*
⅓ cup HELLMANN'S® or BEST FOODS® Real Mayonnaise
¼ cup grated Parmesan cheese
6 boneless, skinless chicken breast halves (about 1¾ pounds)
2 tablespoons plain dry bread crumbs

*Also terrific with LIPTON® RECIPE SECRETS® Onion Soup Mix.

1. Preheat oven to 400°F. In medium bowl, combine soup mix, mayonnaise and cheese; set aside.

2. On baking sheet, arrange chicken. Evenly top chicken with soup mixture, then evenly sprinkle with bread crumbs.

3. Bake 20 minutes or until chicken is thoroughly cooked.   *Makes 6 servings*

chicky quicky

1 cup SONOMA® Dried Tomato Bits
8 chicken thighs (or breast halves)
Juice of 1 lemon
1 tablespoon rosemary
Salt and black pepper, to taste

Place tomato bits in bottom of baking pan; arrange chicken in one layer on top of tomatoes. Squeeze lemon juice over chicken. Sprinkle rosemary, salt and pepper over chicken.

Cover and bake at 350°F until tender, about 40 to 45 minutes. Before serving, spoon juices over top of chicken.
Makes 4 servings

pecan 'n cheese-crusted chicken

½ **cup HELLMANN'S® or BEST FOODS® Real Mayonnaise**
¼ **cup crumbled blue cheese (about 1 ounce)**
¼ **cup chopped toasted pecans**
 4 **boneless, skinless chicken breast halves (about 1¼ pounds)**
 4 **teaspoons Italian seasoned dry bread crumbs**

1. Preheat oven to 425°F.

2. In medium bowl, combine Hellmann's or Best Foods Real Mayonnaise, cheese and pecans. On baking sheet, arrange chicken. Evenly top with mayonnaise mixture, then sprinkle with bread crumbs.

3. Bake 20 minutes or until chicken is thoroughly cooked.   *Makes 4 servings*

Parmesan 'n Pine Nut-Crusted Chicken: Use toasted pine nuts and shredded Parmesan cheese instead of pecans and blue cheese.

Prep Time: 10 minutes
Cook Time: 20 minutes

 tip | Proper wrapping and storage help keep raw cooked chicken at top quality. Refrigerate fresh chicken in its original package on a low shelf in the coldest part of the refrigerator for up to 2 days. Freeze uncooked chicken if it will not be used within 2 days. Also, keep chicken separate from other foods by placing it in a plastic bag or putting it on a pan so it will not drip into other foods.

easy dinners

saffron chicken & vegetables

2 tablespoons vegetable oil

6 bone-in chicken thighs, skinned

1 bag (16 ounces) frozen mixed vegetables, such as broccoli, red bell peppers, mushrooms and onions, thawed

1 can (about 14 ounces) roasted garlic-flavored chicken broth

1 can (10¾ ounces) condensed cream of chicken soup, undiluted

1 can (10¾ ounces) condensed cream of mushroom soup, undiluted

1 package (about 8 ounces) uncooked saffron yellow rice mix with seasonings

½ cup water

1 teaspoon paprika (optional)

1. Preheat oven to 350°F. Spray 3-quart casserole with nonstick cooking spray; set aside.

2. Heat oil in large skillet over medium heat. Brown chicken on both sides; drain fat.

3. Meanwhile, combine vegetables, chicken broth, soups, rice mix with seasonings and water in large bowl. Place mixture in prepared casserole. Top with chicken. Sprinkle with paprika. Cover; bake 1½ hours or until chicken is cooked through (180°F.). *Makes 6 servings*

garlicky baked chicken

1½ cups fresh bread crumbs

3 cloves garlic, minced

1 tablespoon peanut or vegetable oil

2 tablespoons soy sauce

1 tablespoon Chinese hot mustard

1 broiler-fryer chicken, cut up (about 3½ pounds) *or* 3½ pounds chicken parts, skinned, if desired

1. Preheat oven to 350°F. Line baking sheet with foil. Combine bread crumbs, garlic and oil in shallow dish.

2. Combine soy sauce and mustard in small bowl; brush evenly over chicken. Dip chicken in bread crumb mixture to coat evenly and lightly. Place on prepared baking sheet. Bake chicken 45 to 55 minutes or until chicken is cooked through (180°F). *Makes 4 to 6 servings*

saffron chicken & vegetables

double-quick mozzarella chicken

Nonstick cooking spray
4 boneless chicken breasts (about 1 pound)
½ medium lemon or lime
1 teaspoon ground cumin
Salt
¾ cup (3 ounces) shredded mozzarella cheese
½ can (10 ounces) diced Mexican-style tomatoes with chiles, well-drained
   (reserve remaining tomatoes for future use)
2 tablespoons chopped cilantro leaves (optional)

1. Preheat oven to 400°F. Coat baking sheet with cooking spray. Arrange chicken on baking sheet about 2 inches apart. Squeeze lemon juice evenly over the chicken. Sprinkle with cumin and salt. Bake 20 minutes.

2. Sprinkle cheese evenly over chicken; bake an additional 5 minutes or until chicken is no longer pink in center. Transfer chicken to serving platter. Spoon diced tomatoes evenly over chicken. Sprinkle evenly with cilantro. *Makes 4 servings*

 tip | Always cook chicken well done, not medium or rare. If using a meat thermometer, the internal temperature should reach 180°F for whole chicken, 170°F for bone-in parts and 160°F for boneless parts.

pesto-coated baked chicken

   1 pound boneless skinless chicken breasts, cut into ½-inch-thick cutlets
   ¼ cup plus 1 tablespoon prepared pesto
1½ teaspoons sour cream
1½ teaspoons mayonnaise
   1 tablespoon shredded Parmesan cheese
   1 tablespoon pine nuts

1. Preheat oven to 450°F. Arrange chicken in single layer in shallow baking pan. Combine pesto, sour cream and mayonnaise in small cup. Brush over chicken. Sprinkle with cheese and pine nuts.

2. Bake 8 to 10 minutes or until chicken is no longer pink in center.   *Makes 4 servings*

Variation: Chicken can be cooked on an oiled grid over a preheated grill.

ranch chicken pizza

   ½ cup HIDDEN VALLEY® The Original Ranch® Salad Dressing
   1 package (3 ounces) cream cheese, softened
   2 tablespoons tomato paste
   1 cup chopped cooked chicken
   1 (12-inch) prebaked pizza crust
   ½ cup roasted red pepper strips, rinsed and drained
   1 can (2¼ ounces) sliced ripe olives, drained
   ¼ cup chopped green onions
   1 cup (4 ounces) shredded mozzarella cheese

Preheat oven to 450°F. Beat dressing, cream cheese and tomato paste until smooth. Stir in chicken; spread mixture on pizza crust. Arrange red peppers, olives and onions on pizza; sprinkle with mozzarella cheese. Bake at 450°F. for 15 minutes or until hot and bubbly.   *Makes 8 servings*

chicken with piquant raspberry sauce

4 boneless skinless chicken breasts (about 6 ounces each)*
½ teaspoon salt
¼ teaspoon freshly ground black pepper
1½ teaspoons unsalted butter
1½ teaspoons olive oil
½ cup chicken broth
2 tablespoons balsamic vinegar
2 teaspoons prepared mustard
¼ cup seedless raspberry jam

*If chicken cutlets are available, substitute 8 cutlets (about 1½ pounds).

1. Season chicken with salt and pepper. Heat butter and olive oil in large nonstick skillet over medium-high heat.

2. Add chicken; cook 10 to 12 minutes, turning once, or until no longer pink in center. Remove chicken; keep warm.

3. Blend chicken broth, vinegar and mustard; add to pan. Simmer over medium-high heat until sauce is reduced by half. Add raspberry jam; continue cooking until jam has melted and sauce is reduced to about ⅓ cup. Serve sauce with chicken.

Makes 4 servings

oven barbecue chicken

   1 cup barbecue sauce
   ¼ cup honey
   2 tablespoons soy sauce
   2 teaspoons grated fresh ginger
   ½ teaspoon dry mustard
   1 chicken, cut up (about 3½ pounds)

1. Preheat oven to 350°F. Combine barbecue sauce, honey, soy sauce, ginger and mustard in small bowl; mix well.

2. Place chicken in lightly greased baking dish. Brush evenly with sauce mixture. Bake chicken 45 minutes or until cooked through (180°F). Brush with sauce occasionally.   *Makes 4 to 6 servings*

Prep Time: 5 minutes
Cook Time: 45 minutes

quick chicken stew with biscuits

   1 can (10¾ ounces) cream of roasted chicken soup with savory herbs
   1 bag (16 ounces) frozen Southwestern or Mexican-style vegetables
   1 package (10 ounces) PERDUE® SHORT CUTS® Fully Cooked Carved Chicken Breast, Honey Roasted
   1 package (8 ounces) shredded Mexican cheese or Monterey Jack cheese (2 cups), divided
   1½ cups buttermilk baking mix
   ½ cup milk

Preheat oven to 425°F. In lightly greased 12×8-inch baking dish, combine soup and ½ soup can water. Stir in vegetables, chicken and 1 cup cheese. Cover and bake 20 minutes. Meanwhile, in mixing bowl, combine baking mix, remaining 1 cup cheese and milk; stir with fork until all of baking mix is moistened. Spoon baking mix on top of chicken mixture. Bake 15 to 20 minutes, until biscuit topping is golden brown and sauce is hot and bubbly.   *Makes 4 to 6 servings*

Prep Time: 10 minutes
Cook Time: 35 to 40 minutes

jalapeño-lime chicken

8 chicken thighs
3 tablespoons jalapeño jelly
1 tablespoon olive oil
1 tablespoon lime juice
1 clove garlic, minced
1 teaspoon chili powder
½ teaspoon black pepper
⅛ teaspoon salt

1. Preheat oven to 400°F. Line 15×10-inch jelly-roll pan with foil; spray with nonstick cooking spray.

2. Arrange chicken in single layer in prepared pan. Bake 15 minutes; drain off juices. Combine jelly, oil, lime juice, garlic, chili powder, pepper and salt in small bowl. Turn chicken; brush with half of jelly mixture. Bake 20 minutes. Turn chicken; brush with remaining jelly mixture. Bake chicken 10 to 15 minutes or until cooked through (180°F).

Makes 8 servings

Prep Time: 10 minutes
Cook Time: 55 minutes

tip | Boneless skinless chicken thighs can be used in place of boneless breasts in many recipes. Chicken leg meat—legs, thighs and drumsticks—has a rich flavor and is also a great value.

grilled chicken and fresh salsa wraps

1¼ cups LAWRY'S® Herb & Garlic Marinade With Lemon Juice, divided
4 boneless, skinless chicken breasts (about 1 pound)
1 large tomato, chopped
1 can (4 ounces) diced green chiles, drained (optional)
¼ cup thinly sliced green onions
1 tablespoon red wine vinegar
1 tablespoon chopped fresh cilantro
½ teaspoon LAWRY'S® Garlic Salt
4 burrito size *or* 8 fajita size flour tortillas, warmed to soften

In large resealable plastic bag, combine 1 cup Herb & Garlic Marinade and chicken; seal bag and marinate in refrigerator at least 30 minutes. In medium bowl, combine tomato, chiles, onions, remaining ¼ cup Herb & Garlic Marinade, vinegar, cilantro and Garlic Salt; mix well. Cover and refrigerate 30 minutes or until chilled. Remove chicken from bag, discarding used marinade. Grill or broil chicken about 10 to 15 minutes, or until thoroughly cooked, turning halfway through grilling time. Slice chicken into strips. Place chicken on tortillas; spoon salsa mixture on top and wrap to enclose. Serve immediately.   *Makes 4 servings*

Meal Idea: This is an excellent recipe for picnics and outdoor dining. Wrap each filled tortilla with plastic wrap and keep chilled until ready to serve. You may also choose to assemble wraps when ready to serve outdoors!

Prep Time: 12 to 15 minutes
Marinate Time: 30 minutes
Cook Time: 10 to 15 minutes

grilled chicken and
fresh salsa wrap

blue cheese stuffed chicken breasts

½ cup (2 ounces) crumbled blue cheese
2 tablespoons butter, softened, divided
¾ teaspoon dried thyme
  Salt and black pepper
4 bone-in chicken breasts with skin
1 tablespoon lemon juice
½ teaspoon paprika

1. Prepare grill for grilling. Combine blue cheese, 1 tablespoon butter and thyme in small bowl until blended. Season with salt and pepper.

2. Loosen skin over chicken breasts by pushing fingers between skin and meat, taking care not to tear skin. Spread equal amount of blue cheese mixture under skin with rubber spatula or small spoon; massage skin to evenly spread cheese mixture.

3. Place chicken, skin side down, on grid over medium coals. Grill, covered, 10 to 15 minutes. Meanwhile, melt remaining 1 tablespoon butter; stir in lemon juice and paprika. Turn chicken; brush with lemon juice mixture. Grill 15 to 20 minutes more or until chicken is cooked through (170°F). *Makes 4 servings*

Prep and Cook Time: 22 minutes

tip | When buying chicken, the package weight helps determine how much chicken to buy. One pound of raw bone-in chicken serves two or three people, while one pound of raw boneless skinless breasts, tenders or thighs serves up to four.

garlic & lemon herb marinated chicken

  3 to 4 pounds bone-in chicken pieces, skinned if desired
⅓ cup *French's®* Honey Dijon Mustard
⅓ cup lemon juice
⅓ cup olive oil
  3 cloves garlic, minced
  1 tablespoon grated lemon zest
  1 tablespoon minced fresh thyme or rosemary
  1 teaspoon coarse salt
½ teaspoon coarse black pepper

1. Place chicken into resealable plastic food storage bag. Combine remaining ingredients. Pour over chicken. Marinate in refrigerator 1 to 3 hours.

2. Remove chicken from marinade. Grill chicken over medium direct heat for 35 to 45 minutes until juices run clear near bone (170°F for breast meat; 180°F for dark meat). Serve with additional mustard on the side.

Makes 4 servings

Tip: This marinade is also great on whole chicken or pork chops.

Prep Time: 10 minutes
Cook Time: 45 minutes
Marinate Time: 1 hour

lime-mustard marinated chicken

  2 boneless skinless chicken breasts (about ½ pound)
¼ cup fresh lime juice
  3 tablespoons honey mustard, divided
  2 teaspoons olive oil
¼ teaspoon ground cumin
⅛ teaspoon garlic powder
⅛ teaspoon ground red pepper
¾ cup plus 2 tablespoons chicken broth, divided
¼ cup uncooked rice
  1 cup broccoli florets
⅓ cup matchstick carrots

1. Place chicken in resealable food storage bag. Whisk together lime juice, 2 tablespoons mustard, olive oil, cumin, garlic powder and red pepper. Pour over chicken. Seal bag; turn to coat. Marinate in refrigerator 2 hours.

2. Combine ¾ cup chicken broth, rice and remaining 1 tablespoon mustard in small saucepan. Bring to a boil over high heat. Reduce heat. Cover; simmer 12 minutes or until rice is almost tender. Stir in broccoli, carrots and remaining 2 tablespoons chicken broth. Cook, covered, 2 to 3 minutes more or until vegetables are crisp-tender and rice is tender.

3. Meanwhile, prepare grill for direct grilling. Drain chicken; discard marinade. Grill over medium coals 10 to 13 minutes or until no longer pink in center. Serve chicken with rice mixture. *Makes 2 servings*

cajun grilled chicken

4 boneless skinless chicken breast halves
2 tablespoons lemon juice
3 tablespoons MRS. DASH® Extra Spicy Seasoning Blend
2 tablespoons paprika
1 tablespoon brown sugar
   Cooking spray

Preheat grill to medium-high. With a sharp knife, slash each piece of chicken in 2 or 3 places with ¼-inch-deep cuts. In a bowl, combine chicken and lemon juice, turning the chicken until it is thoroughly coated. Set aside. In separate bowl, mix Mrs. Dash® Extra Spicy Seasoning, paprika and brown sugar. Take each piece of chicken and roll in the spice mixture until well coated. Spray grill with cooking spray and place seasoned chicken breasts on the grill. Cook 5 minutes and turn. Cook 5 minutes more or until juices run clear when a skewer is inserted. Serve immediately. *Makes 4 servings*

citrus barbecue chicken

½ cup prepared barbecue sauce
1 teaspoon grated orange peel
1 teaspoon grated fresh ginger
5 boneless, skinless chicken breasts
1 can (20 ounces) DOLE® Pineapple Slices

- Preheat electric grill for 5 minutes.

- Stir together barbecue sauce, orange peel and ginger in small bowl.

- Place chicken breasts on grill, brushing with one-half sauce; close lid. Cook 4 minutes. Turn chicken over and brush with sauce; close lid. Cook 2 more minutes. Add pineapple slices to grill; brush with remaining sauce. Cook 2 more minutes or until chicken is no longer pink in center and slices are lightly browned. Serve each chicken with 2½ pineapple slices. Serve with broccoli florets and rice, if desired. *Makes 5 servings*

rustic grilled chicken sandwich

1 pound boneless chicken breasts, thinly sliced

¾ cup *French's® Gourmayo™* Creamy Dijon Flavored Light Mayonnaise or *French's® Gourmayo™* Caesar Ranch Flavored Light Mayonnaise

3 tablespoons lemon juice

3 tablespoons minced fresh herbs (parsley, basil, thyme or any combination)

1 loaf artisan or rustic-style bread, split in half (remove excess dough from insides)

2 cups mixed field greens or baby spinach

1 (7-ounce) jar sun-dried tomatoes packed in oil, drained and cut into slivers

1. Place chicken into resealable plastic food storage bag. Combine mayonnaise, lemon juice and herbs. Pour ¾ cup mixture over chicken in bag. Seal bag; shake to coat chicken evenly. Marinate in refrigerator 30 minutes or up to 1 hour.

2. Grill or broil chicken 5 to 8 minutes until no longer pink in center.

3. Spread remaining mayonnaise mixture on both sides of bread. Layer field greens and tomatoes on bottom half of bread. Top with chicken pieces and cover with top half of bread. Cut into quarters to serve.

Makes 4 servings

Note: May substitute 1 pound boneless, skinless chicken breasts, pounded to ¼-inch thickness.

Prep Time: 10 minutes
Cook Time: 8 minutes
Marinate Time: 30 minutes

cumin bbq chicken

1 cup prepared barbecue sauce
½ cup orange juice
3 tablespoons vegetable oil
2 tablespoons minced garlic
2 teaspoons ground coriander
2 teaspoons ground cumin
1 teaspoon black pepper
½ teaspoon salt
2 whole chickens (about 3½ pounds each), cut up

1. Combine barbecue sauce, orange juice, oil, garlic, coriander, cumin, black pepper and salt in medium bowl; mix well. Reserve ¾ cup sauce.

2. Prepare grill for direct cooking. Grill chicken over medium coals 10 minutes on each side. Brush lightly with sauce. Grill about 20 minutes more or until chicken is cooked through (180°F).

3. Serve with reserved ¾ cup sauce.

Makes 8 servings

Oven Method: Preheat oven to 375°F. Place chicken in large foil-lined shallow roasting pan. Prepare sauce; reserve ¾ cup. Brush chicken with remaining sauce. Bake 45 to 50 minutes or until chicken cooked through (180°F). Baste chicken with sauce every 15 minutes. *Do not baste during last 5 minutes of baking.* Discard any remaining basting sauce. Serve with reserved ¾ cup sauce.

 tip | When grilling chicken parts, be aware that the various pieces have different cooking times. Check for doneness with a meat thermometer. Bone-in breast parts should reach 170°F and bone-in leg parts 180°F. To check for doneness without a thermometer, pierce the thickest part of the chicken with a fork. It should feel tender and juices should run clear.

thai grilled chicken

4 boneless skinless chicken breasts (about 1¼ pounds)
¼ cup soy sauce
2 teaspoons minced garlic
½ teaspoon red pepper flakes
2 tablespoons honey
1 tablespoon fresh lime juice

1. Prepare grill for direct cooking. Place chicken in shallow baking dish. Combine soy sauce, garlic and pepper flakes. Pour over chicken, turning to coat. Let stand 10 minutes.

2. Meanwhile, combine honey and lime juice in small bowl; blend well. Set aside.

3. Place chicken on grid over medium coals; brush with marinade. Discard remaining marinade. Grill, covered, 5 minutes. Brush both sides of chicken with honey mixture. Grill 5 minutes more or until chicken is no longer pink in center. *Makes 4 servings*

Prep and Cook Time: 25 minutes

bbq yogurt marinated chicken

1 cup STONYFIELD FARM® Yogurt
¼ cup olive oil
2 tablespoons lemon juice
2 cloves garlic, chopped
1 tablespoon dried rosemary
1 tablespoon dried thyme
1 teaspoon salt
1 teaspoon black pepper
4 chicken breasts, skinless, boneless

Combine all ingredients except chicken in bowl; add chicken breasts and marinate in refrigerator for at least 2 hours. Grill chicken on medium-high and serve with potato salad, grilled corn, or any other favorite summer side dishes. *Makes 4 servings*

grilled chicken with chimichurri salsa

4 boneless skinless chicken breasts (6 ounces each)
½ cup plus 4 teaspoons olive oil, divided
   Salt and black pepper
½ cup finely chopped parsley
¼ cup white wine vinegar
2 tablespoons finely chopped onion
3 cloves garlic, minced
1 fresh or canned jalapeño pepper,* finely chopped
2 teaspoons dried oregano

*Jalapeño peppers can sting and irritate the skin, so wear rubber gloves when handling peppers and do not touch eyes.

1. Prepare grill for direct cooking.

2. Brush chicken with 4 teaspoons olive oil; season with salt and black pepper. Place on oiled grid. Grill, covered, over medium heat 5 to 8 minutes on each side or until chicken is no longer pink in center.

3. For salsa, combine parsley, remaining ½ cup olive oil, vinegar, onion, garlic, jalapeño pepper, oregano and salt and black pepper to taste. Serve over chicken. *Makes 4 servings*

tip | Chimichurri salsa has a fresh green color. Serve it with grilled steak or fish as well as chicken. Chimichurri will remain fresh tasting for 24 hours.

grilled sienna chicken

¼ cup lemon juice
2 tablespoons olive oil
1 teaspoon dried basil
¾ teaspoon lemon pepper, divided
1 pound boneless skinless chicken breasts (about 4)
1 cup diced tomatoes
½ teaspoon salt
3 cups arugula or red lettuce leaves, washed

1. Combine lemon juice, oil, basil and ½ teaspoon lemon pepper in small bowl. Place chicken and 3 tablespoons marinade in resealable plastic food storage bag. Seal bag; marinate in refrigerator 1 to 2 hours. Reserve remaining marinade.

2. Combine tomatoes, salt and remaining ¼ teaspoon lemon pepper in small bowl; set aside. Prepare grill for direct grilling.

3. Drain chicken; discard marinade. Grill chicken 15 to 20 minutes or until no longer pink in center, turning and brushing with reserved marinade. Slice chicken; arrange on bed of arugula. Top with tomato mixture.

Makes 4 servings

The publisher would like to thank the companies and organizations listed below for the use of their recipes and photographs in this publication.

Alouette® Cheese, Chavrie® Cheese, Saladena®, Montrachet®

BelGioioso® Cheese Inc.

Birds Eye Foods

Delmarva Poultry Industry, Inc.

Del Monte Corporation

Dole Food Company, Inc.

Equal® sweetener

The Golden Grain Company®

Heinz North America

The Hidden Valley® Food Products Company

Hillshire Farm®

Hormel Foods, LLC

Lee Kum Kee (USA) Inc.

MASTERFOODS USA

Mrs. Dash®

Mushroom Council

National Chicken Council / US Poultry & Egg Association

Newman's Own, Inc.®

Ortega®, A Division of B&G Foods, Inc.

Perdue Farms Incorporated

Reckitt Benckiser Inc.

Sargento® Foods Inc.

Sonoma® Dried Tomatoes

Stonyfield Farm®

Unilever

acknowledgments

154

A

Apple
Pantry Fruited Chicken, 102
Spicy Chicken Apple Salad, 48

Artichokes
Colossal Chicken Salad, 40
Creamy Chicken & Artichoke Quesadillas, 4
Asian Noodles with Vegetables and Chicken, 84

Avocado
Chicken Taco Salad Wraps, 26
Cobb Salad, 44
Santa Fe BBQ Ranch Salad, 50

B

Bacon
Bacon-Wrapped BBQ Chicken, 4
Cobb Salad, 44
Santa Fe BBQ Ranch Salad, 50
Spinach Salad with Bacon Parmesan Dressing, 62
Balsamic Chicken Salad, 44
BBQ Chicken Tacos, 112
BBQ Yogurt Marinated Chicken, 148

Beans
Chicken and Black Bean Chili, 32
Country Chicken and Biscuits, 112
Easy Cajun Chicken Stew, 70
Mexican Tortilla Stacks, 3
Noodly Chicken & Green Bean Skillet, 94
Outrageous Mexican Chicken Salad, 56
Southwest Caesar Salad, 46

Beans *(continued)*
Tortilla "Pizza," 18
White Chicken Chili, 38
Zesty Chicken Succotash, 64
Belgioioso® Kasseri Chicken, 96
Blue Cheese Stuffed Chicken Breasts, 136

Broccoli
Chicken & Broccoli with Garlic Sauce, 72
Creamy Chicken & Broccoli Alfredo, 88
15-Minute Chicken and Broccoli Rice, 66
Garden Ranch Linguine with Chicken, 66
Lime-Mustard Marinated Chicken, 140
Buffalo Chicken Salad Italiano, 42
Buffalo Chicken Tenders, 20

C

Casseroles
Cheesy Chicken Pot Pie, 110
Chili-Chicken Enchiladas, 106
Country Chicken and Biscuits, 112
Garlic Chicken Melt, 102
Green Chile-Chicken Casserole, 108
Quick Chicken Stew with Biscuits, 128
Saffron Chicken & Vegetables, 120

Chicken, Bone-In Pieces
Cumin BBQ Chicken, 146
Garlic & Lemon Herb Marinated Chicken, 138

Chicken, Bone-In Pieces *(continued)*
Garlicky Baked Chicken, 120
Greek Chicken, 114
Honey Lime Glazed Chicken, 110
Oven Barbecue Chicken, 128
Pantry Fruited Chicken, 102
Ranch Crispy Chicken, 100
Roast Chicken with Peppers, 100
Saffron Chicken & Vegetables, 120
Southern BBQ Chicken and Rice, 68
Tandoori Chicken Drumsticks, 132
Zesty Chicken Succotash, 64

Chicken, Boneless Breasts
BBQ Yogurt Marinated Chicken, 148
Belgioioso® Kasseri Chicken, 96
Blue Cheese Stuffed Chicken Breasts, 136
Cajun Grilled Chicken, 142
Cantonese Chicken Stir-Fry, 80
Cashew Chicken, 63
Catalonian Stew, 104
Cheesy Chicken Pot Pie, 110
Chicken and Asparagus Stir-Fry, 68
Chicken and Blue Cheese on Pumpernickel, 22
Chicken & Broccoli with Garlic Sauce, 72
Chicken and Linguine in Creamy Tomato Sauce, 88
Chicken & Mushrooms with Pasta & Roasted Garlic Sauce, 72

index

155

Chicken, Boneless Breasts
(continued)
Chicken and Vegetable Pasta, 132
Chicken Kabobs with Thai Dipping Sauce, 6
Chicken Marengo, 77
Chicken Pomodoro with Tomato Basil Garlic, 81
Chicken Seville, 94
Chicken Taco Salad Wraps, 26
Chicken with Piquant Raspberry Sauce, 126
Chicken with Tomato-Basil Cream Sauce, 82
Chili Cranberry Chicken, 96
Citrus Barbecue Chicken, 142
Citrus-Berry Chicken Salad, 52
Country Chicken and Biscuits, 112
Crispy Garlic Chicken, 116
Double-Quick Mozzarella Chicken, 122
Easy Chicken and Mushroom Stroganoff, 98
Garlic Chicken Melt, 102
Gazebo Chicken, 60
Ginger Plum Chicken, 74
Grilled Chicken and Fresh Salsa Wraps, 134
Grilled Chicken with Chimichurri Salsa, 150
Grilled Sienna Chicken, 152
Honey-Glazed Chicken, 81
Jazzy Jambalaya, 64
Lime-Mustard Marinated Chicken, 140
Nachos con Queso y Cerveza, 8
Noodly Chicken & Green Bean Skillet, 94

Chicken, Boneless Breasts
(continued)
Northwoods Mushroom Swiss Melts, 80
Parmesan 'n Pine Nut-Crusted Chicken, 118
Pecan 'n Cheese-Crusted Chicken, 118
Pesto Chicken-Fontina Crostini, 14
Pesto-Coated Baked Chicken, 124
Rustic Grilled Chicken Sandwich, 144
Salsa Corn Soup with Chicken, 34
Santa Fe BBQ Ranch Salad, 50
Seared Chicken with Greek Salsa, 95
Skillet Chicken, Mushrooms and Vegetables, 90
Southern Style Mustard BBQ Chicken Kabobs, 131
Spanish Skillet Supper, 92
Sweet & Sour Stir-Fry, 78
Thai Grilled Chicken, 148
Walnut Chicken Pinwheels, 14
Zesty Chicken & Vegetable Soup, 36

Chicken, Canned
Creamy Chicken & Broccoli Alfredo, 88
Spicy Chicken & Cheese Quesadillas, 15
Tortilla "Pizza," 18

Chicken, Fully Cooked
Asian Noodles with Vegetables and Chicken, 84
Balsamic Chicken Salad, 44
BBQ Chicken Tacos, 112

Chicken, Fully Cooked *(continued)*
Chicken Florentine in Minutes, 86
Chicken Pasta Salad Supreme, 54
Chicken Salad, 62
Chicken Tortellini Soup, 38
Chicken Tortilla Roll-Ups, 24
Chicken Tortilla Soup, 29
Chili-Chicken Enchiladas, 106
Chinese Chicken Salad, 48
Cobb Salad, 44
Colossal Chicken Salad, 40
Composed Fruit Salad with Chicken, 54
Creamy Chicken & Artichoke Quesadillas, 4
Curried Pasta Salad, 58
Easy Cajun Chicken Stew, 70
15-Minute Chicken and Broccoli Rice, 66
Garden Ranch Linguine with Chicken, 66
Green Chile-Chicken Casserole, 108
Larry's Pineapple Hula Salad, 52
Mexican Tortilla Stacks, 3
Mild Curry Chicken Salad with Fruit, 40
Outrageous Mexican Chicken Salad, 56
Party Chicken Tarts, 28
Pineapple Chicken Salad, 42
Quick Chicken Stew with Biscuits, 128
Quick Hot and Sour Chicken Soup, 34
Ranch Baked Quesadillas, 16
Ranch Chicken Pizza, 124
Refreshing Chicken & Rice Salad, 60
Southwest Caesar Salad, 46

Chicken, Fully Cooked (continued)
Spicy Chicken Apple Salad, 48
Spinach Salad with Bacon Parmesan Dressing, 62
Stuffed Mushroom Caps, 10
30-Minute Paella, 78

Chicken, Ground
Spicy Chicken Bundles, 12
White Chicken Chili, 38

Chicken, Tenders
Bacon-Wrapped BBQ Chicken, 4
Buffalo Chicken Salad Italiano, 42
Buffalo Chicken Tenders, 20
Chicken Caesar Salad, 56
Main-Dish Chicken Soup, 30
Simple Stir-Fry, 86

Chicken, Thighs
Chicken and Black Bean Chili, 32
Chicky Quicky, 116
Coq au Vin & Pasta, 76
Jalapeño-Lime Chicken, 130
Quick Chicken Jambalaya, 92

Chicken, Wings
Cranberry-Barbecue Chicken Wings, 16
Original Ranch® Drummettes, 22

Chili
Chicken and Black Bean Chili, 32
White Chicken Chili, 38
Chili-Chicken Enchiladas, 106
Chili Cranberry Chicken, 96
Chinese Chicken Salad, 48
Citrus Barbecue Chicken, 142
Citrus-Berry Chicken Salad, 52
Cobb Salad, 44

Colossal Chicken Salad, 40
Composed Fruit Salad with Chicken, 54
Coq au Vin & Pasta, 76
Corn
Chicken Tortilla Soup, 29
Salsa Corn Soup with Chicken, 34
Southern BBQ Chicken and Rice, 68
Southwest Caesar Salad, 46
Zesty Chicken Succotash, 64
Country Chicken and Biscuits, 112
Cranberry
Chili Cranberry Chicken, 96
Cranberry-Barbecue Chicken Wings, 16
Pantry Fruited Chicken, 102
Creamy Chicken & Artichoke Quesadillas, 4
Creamy Chicken & Broccoli Alfredo, 88
Crispy Garlic Chicken, 116
Cumin BBQ Chicken, 146
Curried Pasta Salad, 58

D
Double-Quick Mozzarella Chicken, 122

E
Easy Cajun Chicken Stew, 70
Easy Chicken and Mushroom Stroganoff, 98

F
15-Minute Chicken and Broccoli Rice, 66

G
Garden Ranch Linguine with Chicken, 66
Garlic & Lemon Herb Marinated Chicken, 138

Garlic Chicken Melt, 102
Garlicky Baked Chicken, 120
Gazebo Chicken, 60
Ginger Plum Chicken, 74
Greek Chicken, 114
Green Chile-Chicken Casserole, 108
Grilled Chicken and Fresh Salsa Wraps, 134
Grilled Chicken with Chimichurri Salsa, 150
Grilled Sienna Chicken, 152

H
Honey-Glazed Chicken, 81
Honey Lime Glazed Chicken, 110

J
Jalapeño-Lime Chicken, 130
Jazzy Jambalaya, 64

K
Kabobs
Chicken Kabobs with Thai Dipping Sauce, 6
Southern Style Mustard BBQ Chicken Kabobs, 131

L
Larry's Pineapple Hula Salad, 52
Lime-Mustard Marinated Chicken, 140

M
Main-Dish Chicken Soup, 30
Mexican Tortilla Stacks, 3
Mild Curry Chicken Salad with Fruit, 40

index

Mushrooms
    Asian Noodles with Vegetables and Chicken, 84
    Chicken & Mushrooms with Pasta & Roasted Garlic Sauce, 72
    Chicken Marengo, 77
    Chicken Pomodoro with Tomato Basil Garlic, 81
    Coq au Vin & Pasta, 76
    Easy Chicken and Mushroom Stroganoff, 98
    Northwoods Mushroom Swiss Melts, 80
    Party Chicken Tarts, 28
    Skillet Chicken, Mushrooms and Vegetables, 90
    Southern Style Mustard BBQ Chicken Kabobs, 131
    Stuffed Mushroom Caps, 10

N
Nachos con Queso y Cerveza, 8
Noodles (*see also* **Pasta**)
    Asian Noodles with Vegetables and Chicken, 84
    Easy Chicken and Mushroom Stroganoff, 98
    Honey Lime Glazed Chicken, 110
    Noodly Chicken & Green Bean Skillet, 94
    Northwoods Mushroom Swiss Melts, 80
Nuts
    Cashew Chicken, 63
    Chicken Salad, 62
    Chicken Seville, 94
    Larry's Pineapple Hula Salad, 52
    Parmesan 'n Pine Nut-Crusted Chicken, 118

Nuts (*continued*)
    Pecan 'n Cheese-Crusted Chicken, 118
    Spicy Chicken Bundles, 12
    Walnut Chicken Pinwheels, 14

O
Olives
    Colossal Chicken Salad, 40
    Ranch Chicken Pizza, 124
Orange
    Chicken Seville, 94
    Citrus-Berry Chicken Salad, 52
    Cumin BBQ Chicken, 146
    Curried Pasta Salad, 58
    Original Ranch® Drummettes, 22
    Outrageous Mexican Chicken Salad, 56
    Oven Barbecue Chicken, 128

P
Pantry Fruited Chicken, 102
Parmesan 'n Pine Nut-Crusted Chicken, 118
Party Chicken Tarts, 28
Pasta (*see also* **Noodles**)
    Catalonian Stew, 104
    Chicken and Linguine in Creamy Tomato Sauce, 88
    Chicken & Mushrooms with Pasta & Roasted Garlic Sauce, 72
    Chicken and Vegetable Pasta, 132
    Chicken Florentine in Minutes, 86
    Chicken Pasta Salad Supreme, 54
    Chicken Tortellini Soup, 38
    Coq au Vin & Pasta, 76
    Creamy Chicken & Broccoli Alfredo, 88
    Curried Pasta Salad, 58

Pasta (*continued*)
    Garden Ranch Linguine with Chicken, 66
    Noodly Chicken & Green Bean Skillet, 94
    Zesty Chicken & Vegetable Soup, 36
Peas
    Asian Noodles with Vegetables and Chicken, 84
    Chicken Pasta Salad Supreme, 54
    Chicken Salad, 62
    Main-Dish Chicken Soup, 30
    Spanish Skillet Supper, 92
    Sweet & Sour Stir-Fry, 78
    30-Minute Paella, 78
    Pecan 'n Cheese-Crusted Chicken, 118
    Pesto Chicken-Fontina Crostini, 14
    Pesto-Coated Baked Chicken, 124
Pineapple
    Citrus Barbecue Chicken, 142
    Composed Fruit Salad with Chicken, 54
    Curried Pasta Salad, 58
    Honey-Glazed Chicken, 81
    Larry's Pineapple Hula Salad, 52
    Mild Curry Chicken Salad with Fruit, 40
    Pineapple Chicken Salad, 42
Pizza
    Ranch Chicken Pizza, 124
    Tortilla "Pizza," 18

Q
Quesadillas
    Creamy Chicken & Artichoke Quesadillas, 4
    Mexican Tortilla Stacks, 3

Quesadillas *(continued)*
Ranch Baked Quesadillas, 16
Spicy Chicken & Cheese Quesadillas, 15
Quick Chicken Jambalaya, 92
Quick Chicken Stew with Biscuits, 128
Quick Hot and Sour Chicken Soup, 34

R

Ranch Baked Quesadillas, 16
Ranch Chicken Pizza, 124
Ranch Crispy Chicken, 100
Refreshing Chicken & Rice Salad, 60
Rice
Chicken and Asparagus Stir-Fry, 68
Chicken Seville, 94
Easy Cajun Chicken Stew, 70
15-Minute Chicken and Broccoli Rice, 66
Jazzy Jambalaya, 64
Lime-Mustard Marinated Chicken, 140
Northwoods Mushroom Swiss Melts, 80
Quick Chicken Jambalaya, 92
Quick Hot and Sour Chicken Soup, 34
Refreshing Chicken & Rice Salad, 60
Saffron Chicken & Vegetables, 120
Simple Stir-Fry, 86
Southern BBQ Chicken and Rice, 68
Spanish Skillet Supper, 92
30-Minute Paella, 78

Roast Chicken with Peppers, 100
Rustic Grilled Chicken Sandwich, 144

S

Saffron Chicken & Vegetables, 120
Salsa Corn Soup with Chicken, 34
Santa Fe BBQ Ranch Salad, 50
Seared Chicken with Greek Salsa, 95
Shrimp
Jazzy Jambalaya, 64
30-Minute Paella, 78
Simple Stir-Fry, 86
Skillet Chicken, Mushrooms and Vegetables, 90
Slow Cooker
Chicken and Black Bean Chili, 32
Cranberry-Barbecue Chicken Wings, 16
Southern BBQ Chicken and Rice, 68
Southern Style Mustard BBQ Chicken Kabobs, 131
Southwest Caesar Salad, 46
Spanish Skillet Supper, 92
Spicy Chicken & Cheese Quesadillas, 15
Spicy Chicken Apple Salad, 48
Spicy Chicken Bundles, 12
Spinach
Chicken Florentine in Minutes, 86
Chicken Tortellini Soup, 38
Colossal Chicken Salad, 40
Spinach Salad with Bacon Parmesan Dressing, 62
Walnut Chicken Pinwheels, 14
Stuffed Mushroom Caps, 10
Sweet & Sour Stir-Fry, 78

T

Tandoori Chicken Drumsticks, 132
Thai Grilled Chicken, 148
30-Minute Paella, 78
Tortilla "Pizza," 18
Tortillas
Chicken Tortilla Roll-Ups, 24
Chili-Chicken Enchiladas, 106
Creamy Chicken & Artichoke Quesadillas, 4
Green Chile-Chicken Casserole, 108
Grilled Chicken and Fresh Salsa Wraps, 134
Mexican Tortilla Stacks, 3
Ranch Baked Quesadillas, 16
Spicy Chicken & Cheese Quesadillas, 15
Tortilla "Pizza," 18

W

Walnut Chicken Pinwheels, 14
White Chicken Chili, 38
Wraps
Chicken Taco Salad Wraps, 26
Grilled Chicken and Fresh Salsa Wraps, 134
Spicy Chicken Bundles, 12

Z

Zesty Chicken & Vegetable Soup, 36
Zesty Chicken Succotash, 64

index

VOLUME MEASUREMENTS (dry)

$1/8$ teaspoon = 0.5 mL
$1/4$ teaspoon = 1 mL
$1/2$ teaspoon = 2 mL
$3/4$ teaspoon = 4 mL
1 teaspoon = 5 mL
1 tablespoon = 15 mL
2 tablespoons = 30 mL
$1/4$ cup = 60 mL
$1/3$ cup = 75 mL
$1/2$ cup = 125 mL
$2/3$ cup = 150 mL
$3/4$ cup = 175 mL
1 cup = 250 mL
2 cups = 1 pint = 500 mL
3 cups = 750 mL
4 cups = 1 quart = 1 L

VOLUME MEASUREMENTS (fluid)

1 fluid ounce (2 tablespoons) = 30 mL
4 fluid ounces ($1/2$ cup) = 125 mL
8 fluid ounces (1 cup) = 250 mL
12 fluid ounces ($1 1/2$ cups) = 375 mL
16 fluid ounces (2 cups) = 500 mL

WEIGHTS (mass)

$1/2$ ounce = 15 g
1 ounce = 30 g
3 ounces = 90 g
4 ounces = 120 g
8 ounces = 225 g
10 ounces = 285 g
12 ounces = 360 g
16 ounces = 1 pound = 450 g

DIMENSIONS

$1/16$ inch = 2 mm
$1/8$ inch = 3 mm
$1/4$ inch = 6 mm
$1/2$ inch = 1.5 cm
$3/4$ inch = 2 cm
1 inch = 2.5 cm

OVEN TEMPERATURES

250°F = 120°C
275°F = 140°C
300°F = 150°C
325°F = 160°C
350°F = 180°C
375°F = 190°C
400°F = 200°C
425°F = 220°C
450°F = 230°C

BAKING PAN SIZES

Utensil	Size in Inches/Quarts	Metric Volume	Size in Centimeters
Baking or	$8 \times 8 \times 2$	2 L	$20 \times 20 \times 5$
Cake Pan	$9 \times 9 \times 2$	2.5 L	$23 \times 23 \times 5$
(square or	$12 \times 8 \times 2$	3 L	$30 \times 20 \times 5$
rectangular)	$13 \times 9 \times 2$	3.5 L	$33 \times 23 \times 5$
Loaf Pan	$8 \times 4 \times 3$	1.5 L	$20 \times 10 \times 7$
	$9 \times 5 \times 3$	2 L	$23 \times 13 \times 7$
Round Layer	$8 \times 1 1/2$	1.2 L	20×4
Cake Pan	$9 \times 1 1/2$	1.5 L	23×4
Pie Plate	$8 \times 1 1/4$	750 mL	20×3
	$9 \times 1 1/4$	1 L	23×3
Baking Dish	1 quart	1 L	—
or Casserole	$1 1/2$ quart	1.5 L	—
	2 quart	2 L	—

metric conversion chart

15-minute chicken and broccoli rice

1 tablespoon oil
1 small onion, chopped
2 packages (about 9 ounces each) ready-to-serve yellow rice
2 cups frozen chopped broccoli
1 package (about 6 ounces) refrigerated fully cooked chicken breast strips, cut into pieces
½ cup chicken broth or water

1. Heat oil in large skillet over medium-high heat. Add onion; cook 3 minutes or until translucent.

2. Knead rice in bag. Add rice, broccoli, chicken and broth to skillet. Cover; cook 6 to 8 minutes or until hot, stirring occasionally.   *Makes 4 servings*

Serving Suggestion: Top with toasted sliced almonds for a crunchy texture and added flavor.

garden ranch linguine with chicken

8 ounces linguine, cooked and drained
2 cups cooked mixed vegetables, such as broccoli, cauliflower and bell peppers
2 cups cubed cooked chicken
1 cup HIDDEN VALLEY® The Original Ranch® Salad Dressing
1 tablespoon grated Parmesan cheese

Combine all ingredients except cheese in a large saucepan; toss well. Heat through; sprinkle with cheese before serving.   *Makes 4 servings*

15-minute chicken
and broccoli rice

chicken and asparagus stir-fry

        1 cup uncooked rice
        2 tablespoons vegetable oil
        1 pound boneless skinless chicken breasts, cut into ½-inch-wide strips
        2 medium red bell peppers, cut into thin strips
        ½ pound fresh asparagus,* cut diagonally into 1-inch pieces
        ½ cup stir-fry sauce

*For stir-frying, select thin stalks of asparagus.

1. Cook rice according to package directions. Keep hot.

2. Heat oil in wok or large skillet over medium-high heat until hot. Stir-fry chicken 3 to 4 minutes or until chicken is cooked through.

3. Stir in bell peppers and asparagus; reduce heat to medium. Cover; cook 2 minutes or until vegetables are crisp-tender, stirring once or twice.

4. Stir in sauce; heat through. Serve with rice.   *Makes 4 servings*

Prep and Cook Time: 20 minutes

snappy skillets

southern bbq chicken and rice

        1½ cups water
        1 cup UNCLE BEN'S® ORIGINAL CONVERTED® Brand Rice
        1 cup barbecue sauce, divided
        4 skinless bone-in chicken breasts
        1 package (6 half ears) frozen corn-on-the-cob

1. In large skillet, combine water, rice, ¾ cup barbecue sauce and chicken. Bring to a boil. Cover; reduce heat and simmer 25 minutes. Add corn and continue cooking 15 to 20 minutes or until chicken is no longer pink in center.

2. Spoon remaining ¼ cup barbecue sauce over chicken. Remove from heat; let stand 5 minutes or until liquid is absorbed.   *Makes 4 servings*

chicken and asparagus stir-fry

easy cajun chicken stew

2 tablespoons vegetable oil
1 red bell pepper, diced
1 stalk celery, sliced
1 can (about 14 ounces) diced tomatoes with roasted garlic and onions
1½ cups chicken broth
1 package (about 10 ounces) refrigerated fully cooked chicken breast strips, cut into pieces
1 cup canned kidney beans, rinsed and drained
1 pouch (about 9 ounces) New Orleans-style chicken-flavored ready-to-serve rice mix
¼ teaspoon hot pepper sauce
¼ cup chopped green onions

1. Heat oil in Dutch oven over medium-high heat. Add bell pepper and celery. Cook and stir 3 minutes.

2. Add tomatoes and chicken broth; bring to a boil.

3. Add chicken, kidney beans, rice mix and pepper sauce. Reduce heat to low. Cover; cook 7 minutes.

4. Stir in onions. Remove from heat. Cover; let stand 2 to 3 minutes to thicken. *Makes 4 servings*

tip | If canned diced tomatoes with garlic and onions aren't available, substitute 1 can (about 14 ounces) diced tomatoes, 1 teaspoon minced garlic and ¼ cup chopped onions to the bell pepper mixture.

mexican tortilla stacks

½ cup ORTEGA® Salsa, any variety, divided
¼ cup sour cream
½ cup finely chopped cooked chicken
8 (8-inch) ORTEGA Soft Flour Tortillas
½ cup prepared guacamole
⅓ cup ORTEGA Refried Beans
6 tablespoons (1½ ounces) shredded Cheddar cheese
Sour cream and chopped cilantro (optional)

HEAT oven to 350°F. Mix ¼ cup salsa, sour cream and chicken in small bowl.

PLACE 2 tortillas on ungreased cookie sheet; spread with salsa-chicken mixture. Spread 2 more tortillas with guacamole and place on top of salsa-chicken mixture.

MIX refried beans with remaining ¼ cup salsa; spread onto 2 more tortillas and place on top of guacamole. Top each stack with remaining 2 tortillas; sprinkle with cheese.

BAKE 8 to 10 minutes until cheese is melted and filling is hot.

TOP with sour cream and cilantro, if desired. Cut each stack into 8 wedges.   *Makes 16 servings*

Tip: Prepared guacamole can be found in the refrigerated or frozen food sections at most supermarkets.

anytime
appetizers

bacon-wrapped bbq chicken

  8 chicken tender strips, patted dry (about 1 pound)
½ teaspoon paprika or cumin (optional)
  8 slices bacon
½ cup barbecue sauce, divided

1. Preheat broiler. Line broiler pan with foil; set aside.

2. Sprinkle chicken strips with paprika. Wrap each chicken strip with 1 slice of bacon in spiral pattern; place on broiler pan.

3. Broil chicken 4 minutes. Turn chicken over; broil 2 minutes more. Remove from oven; brush with ¼ cup barbecue sauce. Broil about 2 minutes. Remove from oven. Turn over chicken strips; baste with remaining ¼ cup barbecue sauce. Broil 2 minutes more. Serve warm.   *Makes 8 pieces*

creamy chicken & artichoke quesadillas

  1 can (14 ounces) artichoke hearts, drained and chopped
½ cup HELLMANN'S® or BEST FOODS® Real Mayonnaise
½ cup grated Parmesan cheese
1 clove garlic, finely chopped
6 burrito-size flour tortillas
4 ounces cooked chicken, thinly sliced (about 1 cup)
½ cup shredded mozzarella cheese (about 2 ounces)

In medium bowl, combine artichokes, Hellmann's or Best Foods Real Mayonnaise, Parmesan cheese and garlic. Evenly spread mayonnaise mixture on 3 tortillas, then top with chicken, mozzarella cheese and remaining tortillas.

In 12-inch nonstick skillet sprayed with nonstick cooking spray, cook quesadillas over medium-high heat, turning once, 4 minutes or until golden brown and cheese is melted.   *Makes 3 servings*

Prep Time: 10 minutes
Cook Time: 4 minutes

chicken kabobs with thai dipping sauce

1 pound boneless skinless chicken breasts, cut into 1-inch cubes
1 small cucumber, seeded and cut into small chunks
1 cup cherry tomatoes
2 green onions, cut into 1-inch pieces
⅔ cup teriyaki baste & glaze sauce
⅓ cup *Frank's® RedHot®* Original Cayenne Pepper Sauce
⅓ cup peanut butter
3 tablespoons frozen orange juice concentrate, undiluted
2 cloves garlic, minced

1. Thread chicken, cucumber, tomatoes and onions alternately onto metal skewers; set aside.

2. To prepare Thai Dipping Sauce, combine teriyaki baste & glaze sauce, *Frank's RedHot* Sauce, peanut butter, orange juice concentrate and garlic; mix well. Reserve ⅔ cup sauce for dipping.

3. Brush skewers with some of remaining sauce. Place skewers on oiled grid. Grill over hot coals 10 minutes or until chicken is no longer pink in center, turning and basting often with remaining sauce. Serve skewers with reserved Thai Dipping Sauce. Garnish as desired.   *Makes 6 appetizer servings*

Prep Time: 15 minutes
Cook Time: 10 minutes

 tip | When preparing kabobs, be sure to use separate cutting boards for the chicken and vegetables. After cutting up the chicken, properly clean the work area and wash the cutting board in hot soapy water.

nachos con queso y cerveza

28 tortilla chips (4 ounces)
   Nonstick cooking spray
¾ cup chopped red onion
 2 jalapeño peppers,* seeded and chopped
 3 cloves garlic, finely chopped
 2 teaspoons chili powder
½ teaspoon ground cumin
 2 boneless skinless chicken breasts (about 8 ounces), cooked and chopped
 1 can (about 14 ounces) Mexican-style diced tomatoes, drained
⅓ cup pilsner lager
 1 cup (4 ounces) shredded Monterey Jack cheese
 2 tablespoons chopped black olives

*Jalapeño peppers can sting and irritate the skin, so wear rubber gloves when handling peppers and do not touch your eyes.

1. Preheat oven to 350°F. Place chips in 13×9-inch baking pan; set aside.

2. Spray large nonstick skillet with cooking spray. Heat over medium heat until hot. Add onion, peppers, garlic, chili powder and cumin. Cook 5 minutes or until vegetables are tender, stirring occasionally.

3. Stir in chicken, tomatoes and lager. Simmer until liquid is absorbed.

4. Spoon chicken-tomato mixture over chips; top with cheese and olives. Bake 5 minutes or until cheese melts. Serve immediately.   *Makes 4 servings*

stuffed mushroom caps

2 packages (8 ounces each) fresh mushrooms
1 tablespoon butter
⅔ cup finely chopped cooked chicken
¼ cup grated Parmesan cheese
1 tablespoon chopped fresh basil
2 teaspoons lemon juice
⅛ teaspoon onion powder
⅛ teaspoon salt
   Pinch pepper
   Pinch garlic powder
1 small package (3 ounces) cream cheese, softened
   Paprika

1. Preheat oven to 350°F. Clean mushrooms; remove stems and finely chop. Arrange mushroom caps, smooth side down, on greased baking sheet.

2. Melt butter in medium skillet over medium-high heat; cook mushroom stems 5 minutes.

3. Add chicken, Parmesan cheese, basil, lemon juice, onion powder, salt, pepper and garlic powder to skillet. Cook and stir 5 minutes. Remove from heat; stir in cream cheese.

4. Spoon mixture into hollow of each mushroom cap. Bake 10 to 15 minutes until heated through. Sprinkle with paprika. *Makes about 26 stuffed mushrooms*

spicy chicken bundles

1 pound ground chicken or turkey
2 teaspoons minced fresh ginger
2 cloves garlic, minced
¼ teaspoon red pepper flakes
3 tablespoons soy sauce
1 tablespoon cornstarch
1 tablespoon peanut or vegetable oil
⅓ cup finely chopped water chestnuts
⅓ cup thinly sliced green onions
¼ cup chopped peanuts
12 large lettuce leaves, such as romaine
Chinese hot mustard (optional)

1. Combine chicken, ginger, garlic and red pepper flakes in medium bowl. Blend soy sauce into cornstarch in cup until smooth.

2. Heat wok or large skillet over medium-high heat. Add oil; heat until hot. Add chicken mixture; cook and stir 2 to 3 minutes until chicken is cooked through.

3. Stir soy sauce mixture and add to wok. Stir-fry 30 seconds or until sauce boils and thickens. Add water chestnuts, onions and peanuts; heat through.*

4. Divide filling evenly among lettuce leaves; roll up. Secure with toothpicks. Serve warm or at room temperature. Do not let filling stand at room temperature more than 2 hours. Serve with hot mustard.

Makes 12 appetizers

*Filling may be made ahead to this point; cover and refrigerate up to 4 hours. Reheat chicken filling until warm. Proceed as directed in step 4.

spicy chicken bundles

pesto chicken-fontina crostini

1 baguette, cut into 30 (¼-inch-thick) slices
½ (16-ounce) package PERDUE® Fit 'N Easy® Thin Sliced Skinless & Boneless Chicken Breast
      or Turkey Breast Cutlets, cut into 30 pieces
1 tablespoon prepared pesto
¼ teaspoon red pepper flakes
6 ounces fontina, cut into 30 pieces
½ cup roasted red peppers, cut into 1-inch pieces
30 small fresh basil leaves to garnish

Preheat oven to 400°F. Place baguette slices on a baking sheet and toast until golden.

Spray a nonstick skillet with olive oil cooking spray and warm over high heat. Add chicken and sauté until firm and golden. Stir in pesto and red pepper flakes. Set aside.

Place a piece of fontina on each baguette slice and return to oven until cheese melts. Top each crostini with a piece of chicken and a piece of roasted pepper. Garnish with basil leaves and serve.   *Makes 30 crostini*

Prep Time: 30 minutes
Cook Time: 10 minutes

walnut chicken pinwheels

2 boneless skinless chicken breasts, cut into halves
12 to 14 spinach leaves
1 package (6.5 ounces) ALOUETTE® Garlic & Herbs Spreadable Cheese
5 ounces roasted red peppers, sliced or 5 ounces pimiento slices
¾ cup finely chopped California walnuts

Pound chicken to about ¼-inch thickness with flat side of meat mallet or chef's knife. Cover each chicken piece with spinach leaves. Spread each with Alouette®. Top with pepper slices and walnuts. Carefully roll up each breast and secure with wooden toothpicks. Bake at 400°F 20 to 25 minutes until cooked through. Chill. Just before serving, remove toothpicks and slice into ½-inch rounds. Serve cold.

Makes about 35 appetizers

spicy chicken & cheese quesadillas

   8 (10-inch) flour tortillas
   1 cup jalapeño flavored cream cheese*
   1 (10-ounce) can HORMEL® chunk breast of chicken, drained and flaked
1½ cups shredded Monterey Jack and Cheddar cheese
  ⅓ cup diced red bell peppers
  ¼ cup finely chopped red onion
     Mexican toppings such as sour cream, guacamole and salsa

*If unable to locate jalapeño flavored cream cheese in your local supermarket you may make your own (see below).

Spread each flour tortilla with 2 tablespoons cream cheese. In small bowl, combine chicken, shredded cheese, bell peppers and onion. Evenly divide chicken mixture over each of 4 tortillas. Top with remaining flour tortillas. Lightly spray both sides of each quesadilla with nonstick cooking spray. Place quesadillas onto baking sheets. Heat on griddle or in nonstick skillet until golden brown on both sides. Cut quesadillas into wedges and serve with favorite Mexican toppings. *Makes 8 appetizer servings*

For Mild Flavor: Add 1 tablespoon diced jalapeños to 1 cup plain cream cheese

For Medium Flavor: Add 2 to 3 tablespoons diced jalapeños to 1 cup plain cream cheese

For Hot Flavor: Add 1 (4-ounce) can of diced jalapeños to 1 cup plain cream cheese

tip | If you're at a loss for what to make for a last-minute party or an "eat and run" meal, fix quesadillas. They are always popular and can be easily prepared to serve 2 or 20.

15

cranberry-barbecue chicken wings

3 pounds chicken wings
   Salt and black pepper
1 jar (12 ounces) cranberry-orange relish
½ cup barbecue sauce
2 tablespoons quick-cooking tapioca
1 tablespoon prepared mustard

Slow Cooker Directions

1. Preheat broiler. Cut off chicken wing tips; discard. Cut each wing in half at joint. Place chicken on rack in broiler pan; season with salt and pepper. Broil 4 to 5 inches from heat for 10 to 12 minutes or until browned, turning once. Transfer chicken to slow cooker.

2. Stir together relish, barbecue sauce, tapioca and mustard in small bowl. Pour over chicken. Cover; cook on LOW 4 to 5 hours. *Makes about 16 servings*

Prep Time: 20 minutes
Cook Time: 4 to 5 hours

ranch baked quesadillas

1 cup shredded cooked chicken
1 cup (4 ounces) shredded Monterey Jack cheese
½ cup HIDDEN VALLEY® The Original Ranch® Salad Dressing
¼ cup diced green chiles, rinsed and drained
4 (9-inch) flour tortillas, heated
   Salsa and guacamole (optional)

Combine chicken, cheese, dressing and chiles in a medium bowl. Place about ½ cup chicken mixture on each tortilla; fold in half. Place quesadillas on a baking sheet. Bake at 350°F. for 15 minutes or until cheese is melted. Cut into thirds, if desired. Serve with salsa and guacamole, if desired. *Makes 4 servings*

tortilla "pizza"

1 can (about 14 ounces) Mexican-style stewed tomatoes, drained
1 can (10 ounces) chunk white chicken, drained
1 green onion, minced
2 teaspoons ground cumin, divided
½ teaspoon garlic powder
1 cup refried beans
¼ cup chopped fresh cilantro, divided
2 large or 4 small flour tortillas
1 cup (4 ounces) shredded Monterey Jack cheese with jalapeño peppers

1. Preheat broiler. Combine tomatoes and chicken in medium bowl. Add green onion, 1 teaspoon cumin and garlic powder. Mix well; set aside.

2. Mix refried beans, remaining 1 teaspoon cumin and 2 tablespoons cilantro in small bowl. Set aside.

3. Place tortillas on baking sheet. Broil 30 seconds to 1 minute per side or until crisp but not browned. Remove from oven. Decrease oven temperature to 400°F.

4. Spread bean mixture evenly over each tortilla. Spoon chicken mixture over beans; top with cheese. Bake 5 minutes.

5. Turn oven temperature to broil. Broil tortillas 2 to 3 minutes or until cheese melts. Do not let tortilla edges burn. Remove from oven; top with remaining cilantro. Serve immediately. (If using large tortillas, cut each in half.)   *Makes 4 servings*

Prep and Cook Time: 19 minutes

tortilla "pizza"

buffalo chicken tenders

 3 tablespoons Louisiana-style hot sauce
½ teaspoon paprika
¼ teaspoon ground red pepper
 1 pound chicken tenders
½ cup blue cheese dressing
¼ cup sour cream
 2 tablespoons crumbled blue cheese
 1 medium green or red bell pepper, cut lengthwise into ½-inch-thick slices

1. Preheat oven to 375°F. Combine hot sauce, paprika and ground red pepper in small bowl; brush on all surfaces of chicken. Place chicken in greased 11×7-inch baking dish. Cover; marinate in refrigerator 30 minutes.

2. Bake, uncovered, about 15 minutes or until chicken is no longer pink in center.

3. Combine blue cheese dressing, sour cream and blue cheese in small serving bowl. Serve dip with chicken and bell pepper. *Makes 10 servings*

Note: Create two appetizers at once. Double or triple the recipe for the dip and serve with additional crunchy raw vegetables for a simple but delicious party snack.

 tip | If you don't have chicken tenders on hand, simply make your own. Just slice boneless skinless chicken breasts lengthwise into 3 or 4 strips.

original ranch® drummettes

1 packet (1 ounce) HIDDEN VALLEY® The Original Ranch® Salad Dressing & Seasoning Mix
¼ cup vegetable oil
24 chicken drummettes (about 2 pounds)

Combine dressing mix and oil in large bowl. Add drummettes; toss well to coat. Arrange on rack placed in foil-lined baking pan; bake at 425°F for 25 minutes. Turn drummettes over; bake additional 20 minutes.

Makes 24 drummettes

Spicy Hot Variation: Add 2 tablespoons red pepper sauce to dressing mixture before coating.

Serving Suggestion: Dip cooked drummettes in prepared Hidden Valley® Original Ranch® salad dressing.

chicken and blue cheese on pumpernickel

½ (16-ounce) package PERDUE® Fit 'N Easy® Thin-Sliced Skinless & Boneless Chicken Breast or Turkey Breast Cutlets
⅓ cup crumbled blue cheese
¾ tablespoon Dijon mustard
Salt and pepper, to taste
16 slices cocktail pumpernickel, toasted and buttered
½ small red onion, very thinly sliced
1 cup arugula, radicchio or watercress, very thinly sliced

Set a large, non-stick skillet over high heat and coat it with cooking spray. Sauté chicken until golden brown on both sides and cooked through. Set aside to cool.

In a medium bowl, stir together blue cheese and mustard. Dice chicken and stir it in. Season to taste with salt and pepper.

To assemble, top each slice of bread with some onion, a heaping tablespoon of chicken and sprinkle with arugula. Serve immediately.

Make 16 appetizers

Prep Time: 30 minutes
Cook Time: 5 minutes

chicken tortilla roll-ups

4 ounces cream cheese, softened
2 tablespoons mayonnaise
1 tablespoon Dijon mustard
¼ teaspoon black pepper
3 (10- or 12-inch) flour tortillas
1 cup finely chopped cooked chicken
¾ cup shredded or finely chopped carrot
¾ cup finely chopped green bell pepper
3 tablespoons chopped green onion

1. Combine cream cheese, mayonnaise, mustard and black pepper in small bowl; stir until well blended.

2. Spread cream cheese mixture evenly onto each tortilla leaving ½-inch border. Sprinkle chicken, carrot, bell pepper and green onion evenly over cream cheese leaving 1½-inch border on cream cheese mixture at one end of each tortilla.

3. Roll up each tortilla jelly-roll fashion. Cut each roll into 1½-inch-thick slices.

Makes about 18 slices

tip | Roll-ups are great make-ahead appetizers. Wrap rolls in plastic wrap and refrigerate for several hours. The rolls will slice easier and the extra time allows the flavors to blend.

chicken taco salad wraps

  1 ripe large avocado, pitted, peeled and diced
¾ cup peeled and diced jicama
  2 teaspoons lime juice
  2 tablespoons vegetable oil
  1 pound boneless chicken breasts, cut into strips
  1 package (1.25 ounces) ORTEGA® Taco Seasoning Mix
¾ cup water
  8 ORTEGA Taco Shells, coarsely crushed
12 large Bibb lettuce leaves
½ cup (2 ounces) shredded Mexican blend cheese
¼ cup chopped fresh cilantro
  1 jar (8 ounces) ORTEGA Taco Sauce

STIR together avocado and jicama with lime juice in small bowl; set aside.

HEAT oil in large skillet over medium-high heat. Add chicken strips; cook and stir 4 to 6 minutes or until chicken is no longer pink. Stir in taco seasoning mix and water. Bring to a boil. Reduce heat to low; cook for 2 to 3 minutes or until mixture is thickened, stirring occasionally. Remove from heat.

MICROWAVE crushed taco shells on HIGH (100%) 1 minute.

SPOON ⅓ cup chicken filling onto each lettuce leaf; layer with taco shells, avocado mixture, cheese and cilantro. Wrap lettuce around filling and serve with taco sauce. *Makes about 12 wraps*

chicken taco salad wrap

party chicken tarts

1½ **cups chopped cooked chicken**
2 **tablespoons butter or margarine**
1 **cup chopped fresh mushrooms**
¼ **cup finely chopped celery**
¼ **cup finely chopped onion**
2 **tablespoons all-purpose flour**
6 **tablespoons sour cream**
½ **teaspoon garlic salt**
1 **package (10 ounces) flaky refrigerator biscuits (10 to 12 count)**
Vegetable cooking spray
1 **tablespoon butter or margarine, melted**
Grated Parmesan cheese

Melt 2 tablespoons butter in large skillet until hot. Add mushrooms, celery and onion; cook and stir 4 to 5 minutes. Sprinkle with flour; stir in chicken and sour cream. Cook until thoroughly heated. Stir in garlic salt; set aside. Cut each biscuit into quarters; press each piece into miniature muffin tins coated with cooking spray to form tart shell. Brush each piece with melted butter. Bake at 400°F 6 minutes. Remove from oven; reduce oven temperature to 350°F. Fill each tart with 1 teaspoon chicken mixture; sprinkle with cheese. Bake 14 to 15 minutes more. Serve immediately.   *Makes 40 to 48 appetizers*

Note: For ease in serving at party time, prepare filling ahead of time and cook tarts 5 minutes. Fill and bake just before serving for best flavor.

Favorite recipe from **National Chicken Council**

chicken tortilla soup

1 teaspoon oil
1 clove garlic, minced
1 can (14½ ounces) chicken broth
1 jar (16 ounces) mild chunky-style salsa
¾ cup water
2 tablespoons *Frank's® RedHot®* Original Cayenne Pepper Sauce
1 package (10 ounces) fully cooked carved chicken breasts
1 can (8¾ ounces) whole kernel corn, undrained
1 tablespoon chopped fresh cilantro (optional)
1 cup crushed tortilla chips
½ cup (2 ounces) shredded Monterey Jack cheese

1. Heat oil in large saucepan over medium-high heat. Cook garlic 1 minute or until tender. Add broth, salsa, water and *Frank's RedHot* Sauce. Stir in chicken, corn and cilantro. Heat to boiling. Reduce heat to medium-low. Cook, covered, 5 minutes.

2. Stir in tortilla chips and cheese. Serve hot.   *Makes 4 servings*

Prep Time: 5 minutes
Cook Time: 6 minutes

speedy
soups & salads

main-dish chicken soup

  1 can (about 49½ ounces) chicken broth *or* 3 cans (about 14 ounces each) chicken broth
     plus 6 ounces of water
  1 cup grated carrots
  ½ cup sliced green onions
  ½ cup diced red bell pepper
  ½ cup frozen green peas
  1 seedless cucumber
12 chicken tenders (about 1 pound)
  ½ teaspoon white pepper

1. Place broth in large Dutch oven. Bring to a boil over high heat. Add carrots, green onions, bell pepper and peas. Return to a boil. Reduce heat; simmer 3 minutes.

2. Meanwhile, cut ends off cucumber and discard. Using vegetable peeler, start at top and make long, noodle-like strips of cucumber. Slice any remaining cucumber pieces thinly with knife. Add cucumber to Dutch oven; cook 2 minutes over low heat.

3. Add chicken tenders and white pepper; simmer 5 minutes or until chicken is cooked through.

Makes 6 servings

Serving Suggestion: Serve with a small mixed green salad or sliced tomatoes on a bed of lettuce and crusty French bread.

chicken and black bean chili

1 pound boneless skinless chicken thighs, cut into 1-inch chunks
2 teaspoons chili powder
2 teaspoons ground cumin
¾ teaspoon salt
1 green bell pepper, diced
1 small onion, chopped
3 cloves garlic, minced
1 can (about 14 ounces) diced tomatoes, undrained
1 cup chunky salsa
1 can (about 15 ounces) black beans, rinsed and drained
   Optional toppings: sour cream, diced ripe avocado, shredded Cheddar cheese, sliced green onions or chopped cilantro, crushed tortilla or corn chips

Slow Cooker Directions

1. Combine chicken, chili powder, cumin and salt in slow cooker; toss to coat.

2. Add bell pepper, onion and garlic; mix well. Stir in tomatoes and salsa. Cover; cook on LOW 5 to 6 hours or on HIGH 2½ to 3 hours or until chicken is tender.

3. Turn heat to HIGH; stir in beans. Cover; cook 5 to 10 minutes or until beans are heated through. Ladle into shallow bowls; serve with desired toppings.

Makes 4 servings

quick hot and sour chicken soup

2 cups chicken broth

2 cups water

1 package (about 10 ounces) refrigerated fully cooked chicken breast strips, cut into pieces

1 package (about 7 ounces) chicken-flavored rice and vermicelli mix

1 large jalapeño pepper,* minced

2 green onions, chopped

1 tablespoon soy sauce

1 tablespoon fresh lime juice

1 tablespoon minced fresh cilantro (optional)

*Jalapeño peppers can sting and irritate the skin, so wear rubber gloves when handling peppers and do not touch your eyes.

1. Combine broth, water, chicken, rice mix, jalapeño pepper, green onions and soy sauce in large saucepan. Bring to a boil over high heat. Reduce heat to low. Cover; simmer 20 minutes or until rice is tender, stirring occasionally.

2. Stir in lime juice; sprinkle with cilantro.

Makes 4 servings

salsa corn soup with chicken

3 quarts chicken broth

2 pounds boneless skinless chicken breasts, cooked and diced

2 packages (10 ounces each) frozen whole kernel corn, thawed

4 jars (11 ounces each) NEWMAN'S OWN® All Natural Salsa

4 large carrots, diced

Bring chicken broth to a boil in Dutch oven. Add chicken, corn, Newman's Own® Salsa and carrots. Bring to a boil. Reduce heat and simmer until carrots are tender.

Makes 8 servings

quick hot and sour chicken soup

zesty chicken & vegetable soup

½ pound boneless skinless chicken breasts, cut into very thin strips
1 to 2 tablespoons *Frank's® RedHot®* **Original Cayenne Pepper Sauce**
4 cups chicken broth
1 package (16 ounces) frozen stir-fry vegetables
1 cup angel hair pasta, broken into 2-inch lengths *or* **fine egg noodles**
1 green onion, thinly sliced

1. Combine chicken and *Frank's RedHot* Sauce in medium bowl; set aside.

2. Heat broth to boiling in large saucepan over medium-high heat. Add vegetables and pasta; return to boiling. Cook 2 minutes. Stir in chicken mixture and green onion. Cook 1 minute or until chicken is no longer pink.

Makes 4 to 6 servings

Tip: For a change of pace, substitute 6 prepared frozen pot stickers for the pasta. Add to broth in step 2 and boil until tender.

Prep Time: 5 minutes
Cook Time: about 8 minutes

tip | For easier slicing, put the chicken in the freezer for about 1 hour to firm up. Or, if using frozen chicken, slice into thin strips before the chicken is completely thawed. For more tender pieces, be sure to cut the chicken across the grain.

chicken tortellini soup

6 cups chicken broth *or* **1 can (48 ounces) chicken broth**
1 package (9 ounces) refrigerated cheese and spinach tortellini or three-cheese tortellini
1 package (about 6 ounces) refrigerated fully cooked chicken breast strips, cut into bite-size pieces
2 cups coarsely chopped fresh baby spinach leaves
4 to 6 tablespoons grated Parmesan cheese
1 tablespoon chopped chives *or* **2 tablespoons sliced green onions**

1. Bring chicken broth to a boil in large saucepan over high heat. Add tortellini. Reduce heat to medium; cook 5 minutes. Stir in chicken and spinach.

2. Reduce heat to low. Cook 3 minutes or until chicken is hot. Sprinkle with Parmesan cheese and chives.

Makes 4 servings

white chicken chili

1 to 2 tablespoons canola oil
1 onion, chopped (about 1 cup)
1 package (about 1¼ pounds) PERDUE® Fresh Ground Chicken, Turkey or Turkey Breast Meat
1 package (about 1¾ ounces) chili seasoning mix
1 can (14½ ounces) reduced-sodium chicken broth
1 can (15 ounces) cannellini or white kidney beans, drained and rinsed

In Dutch oven over medium-high heat, heat oil. Add onions; sauté 2 to 3 minutes, until softened and translucent. Add ground chicken; sauté 5 to 7 minutes, until no longer pink. Add chili mix and stir to combine. Add chicken broth and beans; bring to a boil. Reduce heat to medium-low; simmer 5 to 10 minutes, until all flavors are blended.

Makes 4 servings

Prep Time: 10 minutes
Cook Time: 10 to 20 minutes

chicken tortellini soup

mild curry chicken salad with fruit

2 cups (1 pint) prepared deli creamy chicken salad
2 teaspoons sugar
1½ to 2 teaspoons curry powder
⅛ teaspoon ground red pepper (optional)
8 slices fresh pineapple, cut into wedges

1. Combine chicken salad, sugar, curry and red pepper in medium bowl. Stir gently to blend thoroughly.

2. Spoon equal amounts salad on 4 plates. Arrange pineapple around salad. *Makes 4 servings*

Variation: Add 2 tablespoons *each* currants, chopped apples, sliced red grapes, sliced green onions and toasted slivered almonds. Serve on a bed of spring greens or baby spinach leaves. Garnish with fresh pineapple chunks.

Tip: Try toasting the curry powder for another flavor. Heat a dry, nonstick skillet over medium-high heat until hot. Add curry; cook about 1 minute, stirring constantly to prevent burning. Immediately remove from skillet.

colossal chicken salad

2 cups cooked chicken strips
1½ cups HIDDEN VALLEY® The Original Ranch® Salad Dressing, divided
½ pound fresh spinach leaves, washed, drained and torn or Romaine lettuce leaves
1 jar (7 ounces) marinated artichoke hearts, drained
1 large red bell pepper, cut into thin strips or 1 large tomato, cut into wedges
1 can (5.7 ounces) pitted black colossal olives, drained
3 tablespoons grated Parmesan cheese

In shallow glass dish, combine chicken and ½ cup of the salad dressing. Cover and refrigerate at least 1 hour. Drain chicken; discard marinade. Arrange spinach leaves on 4 individual salad plates. Divide chicken, artichoke hearts, red pepper and olives evenly among plates. Sprinkle with cheese. Serve remaining 1 cup salad dressing on the side. *Makes 4 servings*

mild curry chicken salad with fruit

buffalo chicken salad italiano

½ cup *Frank's® RedHot®* Buffalo Wing Sauce
½ cup prepared Italian salad dressing
 1 pound frozen chicken tenders, thawed
 8 cups torn salad greens
 1 cup sliced celery
 1 cup crumbled gorgonzola or blue cheese

1. Combine Wing Sauce and salad dressing in bowl. Pour ½ cup mixture over chicken tenders in large bowl. Cover and refrigerate 20 minutes.

2. Cook chicken on electric grill pan or barbecue grill for 3 to 5 minutes until no longer pink in center.

3. Arrange salad greens, celery and cheese on serving plates. Top with chicken and drizzle with remaining Wing Sauce mixture.

Makes 4 servings

Tip: You may substitute 1 pound boneless, skinless chicken breast halves for chicken tenders.

Prep Time: 5 minutes
Cook Time: 5 minutes
Marinate Time: 20 minutes

pineapple chicken salad

 1 packet (1 ounce) HIDDEN VALLEY® The Original Ranch® Salad Dressing & Seasoning Mix
½ cup mayonnaise
¼ cup pineapple juice
 2 cups cubed, cooked chicken
 1 cup sliced celery
 1 can (20 ounces) pineapple chunks (reserve juice for above)

Combine salad dressing and seasoning mix with mayonnaise and pineapple juice. Add chicken, celery and pineapple to mixture and toss well to coat. Chill.

Makes 4 to 6 servings

cobb salad

1 package (10 ounces) torn mixed salad greens *or* 8 cups torn romaine lettuce
6 ounces deli chicken, turkey or smoked turkey breast, cut ¼ inch thick
1 large tomato, seeded and chopped
⅓ cup bacon bits or crumbled crisp-cooked bacon
1 large ripe avocado, peeled and diced
⅓ cup prepared blue cheese or Caesar salad dressing

1. Place lettuce in salad bowl. Dice chicken; place in center of lettuce. Arrange tomato, bacon and avocado in rows on either side of chicken.

2. Drizzle with dressing. Serve immediately.

Makes 4 servings

Prep Time: 15 minutes

balsamic chicken salad

⅓ cup olive oil
¼ cup *French's®* Honey Mustard
2 tablespoons balsamic or red wine vinegar
1 teaspoon minced shallots or onion
8 cups mixed salad greens, washed and torn
1 package (10 ounces) fully cooked carved chicken breasts
1 package (4 ounces) goat or Feta cheese, crumbled
1 cup croutons

1. Whisk together oil, mustard, vinegar, shallots, *2 tablespoons water* and *⅛ teaspoon salt*.

2. Arrange salad greens, chicken, cheese and croutons on serving plates. Serve with dressing.

Makes 4 servings

Prep Time: 10 minutes

cobb salad

southwest caesar salad

1 package (10 ounces) DOLE® Complete Caesar Salad
2 cups cubed cooked chicken breast
1 can (14 to 16 ounces) low-sodium kidney, black or pinto beans, drained
1 can (8 ounces) low-sodium whole kernel corn, drained
1 medium tomato, cut into wedges
1 medium DOLE® Red, Yellow or Green Bell Pepper, thinly sliced
½ medium onion, thinly sliced

- Combine romaine, croutons and Parmesan cheese from salad bag with chicken, beans, corn, tomato, bell pepper and onion in large serving bowl.

- Pour dressing from packet over salad; toss to evenly coat.

Makes 4 servings

Note: Refrigerate salad blends, complete salads and vegetable combinations in their original bags as soon as you get them home. Since the bags have been designed with a special material to keep vegetables at their freshest, you can store any leftovers in the same bags, tightly closed, in your refrigerator crisper.

Prep Time: 10 minutes

 tip | If you're trying to get your family to eat more salad, start with a Caesar salad kit. Make a mini salad bar by putting ingredients—romaine, croutons, chicken, bell peppers, etc—in separate bowls. Let everyone assemble their own salad. They'll be much more likely to eat the salad and you'll be much happier that they ate a nutritious meal.

southwest caesar salad

chinese chicken salad

4 cups chopped bok choy
3 cups cooked diced chicken breast (1 pound boneless skinless chicken breast meat)
1 cup shredded carrots
2 tablespoons minced chives or green onions
2 tablespoons hot chili sauce with garlic*
1½ tablespoons peanut or canola oil
1 tablespoon balsamic vinegar
1 tablespoon soy sauce
1 teaspoon minced fresh ginger

*Hot chili sauce with garlic is available in the Asian foods section of most supermarkets.

1. Place bok choy, chicken, carrots and chives in serving bowl.

2. Combine chili sauce, oil, vinegar, soy sauce and ginger in small bowl; mix well. Pour over chicken mixture; toss gently.

Makes 4 servings

spicy chicken apple salad

¼ cup HELLMANN'S® or BEST FOODS® Canola Real Mayonnaise
¼ cup jalapeño pepper jelly or mango chutney
8 cups mixed salad greens or baby spinach leaves
2 cups cut-up cooked chicken
1 medium Red or Golden Delicious apple, thinly sliced

1. In small bowl, combine Hellmann's or Best Foods Canola Real Mayonnaise with jelly; set aside.

2. To serve, arrange salad greens on serving platter, then top with chicken, apple and reserved mayonnaise mixture.

Makes 4 servings

Tip: Also terrific with Hellmann's® or Best Foods® Light Mayonnaise.

Prep Time: 15 minutes

chinese chicken salad

santa fe bbq ranch salad

1 cup *Cattlemen's*® Golden Honey Barbecue Sauce, divided
½ cup ranch salad dressing
1 pound boneless, skinless chicken
12 cups washed and torn Romaine lettuce
1 small red onion, thinly sliced
1 small ripe avocado, diced ½-inch
4 ripe plum tomatoes, sliced
2 cups shredded Monterey Jack cheese
½ cup cooked, crumbled bacon

1. Prepare BBQ Ranch Dressing: Combine ½ cup barbecue sauce and salad dressing in small bowl; reserve.

2. Grill or broil chicken over medium-high heat 10 minutes until no longer pink in center. Cut into strips and toss with remaining ½ cup barbecue sauce.

3. Toss lettuce, onion, avocado, tomatoes, cheese and bacon in large bowl. Portion on salad plates, dividing evenly. Top with chicken and serve with BBQ Ranch Dressing.   *Makes 4 servings*

Tip: Serve *Cattlemen's*® Golden Honey Barbecue Sauce as a dipping sauce with chicken nuggets or seafood kabobs.

Prep Time: 15 minutes
Cook Time: 10 minutes

citrus-berry chicken salad

    4 boneless skinless chicken breast halves
    ½ cup *French's*® Honey Mustard, divided
    ⅓ cup canola oil
    2 tablespoons raspberry vinegar or balsamic vinegar
    8 cups mixed salad greens, washed and torn
    1 cup sliced strawberries or raspberries
    1 orange, cut into sections

1. Coat chicken with *¼ cup* mustard. Broil or grill 10 to 15 minutes or until chicken is no longer pink in center. Cut diagonally into slices.

2. In small bowl, whisk together remaining *¼ cup* mustard, oil, vinegar and *¼ teaspoon each salt and pepper.*

3. Arrange salad greens and fruit on serving plates. Top with chicken. Drizzle with dressing just before serving.

Makes 4 servings

larry's pineapple hula salad

    2 cans (8 ounces each) DOLE® Pineapple Chunks, drained
    2 cups cubed cooked chicken
    1 cup diagonally sliced celery
    1 cup diced DOLE® Papaya
    ½ cup macadamia nuts or peanuts
    1 cup mayonnaise
    2 teaspoons curry powder
    Crisp salad greens
    Chives and sliced kumquats for garnish

Combine pineapple chunks, chicken, celery, papaya and nuts in large bowl. Blend mayonnaise and curry powder in small bowl; pour over chicken mixture. Blend thoroughly. Cover; chill at least 1 hour. Serve mounded on salad greens. Garnish with chives and kumquats.

Makes 4 servings

citrus-berry chicken salad

chicken pasta salad supreme

3 cups diced cooked chicken
1 package (8 ounces) medium shell pasta, cooked according to package directions, drained
1 medium red pepper, cut in 1½×¼-inch strips
1 package (8 ounces) frozen snow peas, thawed, drained
¼ cup sliced green onion
¾ cup bottled, reduced calorie oil and vinegar dressing
1 cup cherry tomatoes, halved
Lettuce leaves

In a large bowl, place chicken, pasta, red pepper, snow peas and green onion; toss to mix. Pour dressing over chicken mixture; toss to mix. Cover and chill until ready to serve. Add tomatoes; toss gently. Serve on lettuce-lined plates.   *Makes 6 servings*

Favorite recipe from **Delmarva Poultry Industry, Inc.**

composed fruit salad with chicken

2 cooked boneless, skinless chicken breast halves, sliced
1 can (8 ounces) DOLE® Pineapple Chunks, drained
½ DOLE® Papaya, peeled, seeded, sliced
2 small clusters seedless red grapes
2 tablespoons bottled poppy seed dressing
1 tablespoon lime juice
1 tablespoon minced cilantro

● Arrange chicken and fruit on plate.

● Combine salad dressing, lime juice and cilantro. Spoon dressing over chicken and fruit.

Makes 2 servings

Prep Time: 15 minutes

chicken pasta salad supreme

chicken caesar salad

6 ounces chicken tenders

¼ cup plus 1 tablespoon Caesar salad dressing, divided

Black pepper

4 cups (about 5 ounces) prepared Italian salad mix (romaine and radicchio)

½ cup croutons, divided

2 tablespoons grated Parmesan cheese

1. Cut chicken tenders in half lengthwise and crosswise. Heat 1 tablespoon salad dressing in large nonstick skillet. Add chicken; cook and stir over medium heat 3 to 4 minutes or until chicken is cooked through. Remove chicken from skillet. Season with pepper; let cool.

2. Combine salad mix, ¼ cup croutons, remaining ¼ cup salad dressing and Parmesan cheese in serving bowl; toss to coat. Top with chicken and remaining ¼ cup croutons.   *Makes 2 servings*

Prep and Cook Time: 20 minutes

outrageous mexican chicken salad

6 cups shredded lettuce

1 bag (9 ounces) tortilla chips, crushed (about 3 cups)

2 cups cubed cooked chicken

1 can (15½ ounces) kidney beans, rinsed and drained

1½ cups HIDDEN VALLEY® The Original Ranch® Salad Dressing

½ cup (2 ounces) shredded Cheddar cheese

Tomatoes and olives

Combine lettuce, tortilla chips, chicken, beans, dressing and cheese in a large bowl. Garnish with tomatoes and olives.

Makes 4 to 6 servings

chicken caesar salad

curried pasta salad

4 ounces uncooked bow tie or corkscrew (fusilli) pasta
1 can (8 ounces) DOLE® Pineapple Chunks
½ cup fat free or reduced fat mayonnaise
2 teaspoons packed brown sugar
1 teaspoon curry powder
1 can (11 or 15 ounces) DOLE® Mandarin Oranges, drained
1½ cups cooked chicken breast or turkey breast strips
½ cup sliced celery
¼ cup chopped green onions

- Cook pasta as package directs; drain.

- Drain pineapple chunks; reserve 3 tablespoons juice.

- Stir reserved juice, mayonnaise, sugar and curry in large serving bowl until blended.

- Add pasta, pineapple chunks, mandarin oranges, chicken, celery and green onions to curry dressing; toss to evenly coat. Serve on lettuce-lined plate and garnish with shredded red cabbage, if desired.

Makes 4 servings

Prep Time: 10 minutes
Cook Time: 15 minutes

tip | Pasta salads have more flavor at room temperature than cold. Run cold water over hot pasta to cool it, then toss it with the remaining ingredients and dressing—no chilling needed. Or, when using cooked chilled pasta, simply run very hot water over the pasta to warm it up.

curried pasta salad

gazebo chicken

4 boneless chicken breast halves (about 1½ pounds)
6 cups torn butter lettuce leaves or mixed baby greens
1 ripe cantaloupe, seeded and cut into 12 wedges
1 large carrot, shredded
½ cup fresh raspberries
⅔ cup prepared honey-mustard salad dressing, divided

1. Preheat broiler. Place chicken, skin side down, on broiler pan rack. Season with salt and pepper. Broil 4 to 5 inches from heat 8 minutes. Turn; sprinkle with salt and pepper. Broil 6 to 8 minutes or until chicken is no longer pink in center. Remove; cool on broiler pan. Transfer chicken to cutting board. Slice each breast diagonally into thirds.

2. Place lettuce on large serving platter; arrange cantaloupe and carrot around lettuce. Scatter raspberries over salad; drizzle with about 2 tablespoons dressing. Serve with remaining dressing. *Makes 4 servings*

refreshing chicken & rice salad

1 package (4.3 ounces) RICE-A-RONI® Long Grain & Wild Rice Pilaf
1 tablespoon vegetable oil
2 cups chopped cooked chicken
2 carrots, sliced lengthwise, cut into slices
1 cucumber, peeled, seeded, cut into short thin strips
½ cup red or green bell pepper, cut into short thin strips
2 tablespoons sliced green onions
⅓ cup Italian dressing
Lettuce

1. Prepare Rice-A-Roni® Mix as package directs, substituting oil for margarine. Cool 10 minutes.

2. In large bowl, combine prepared Rice-A-Roni®, chicken, carrots, cucumber, bell pepper, onions and dressing. Chill 4 hours or overnight. Stir before serving. Serve on lettuce-lined platter. *Makes 5 servings*

gazebo chicken

spinach salad with bacon parmesan dressing

2 packages (6 ounces each) HILLSHIRE FARM® Deli Select Smoked Chicken Breast
8 cups fresh spinach
2 cups freshly grated Parmesan cheese
⅔ cup extra-virgin olive oil
⅓ cup crumbled cooked bacon
¼ cup white wine vinegar or balsamic vinegar
3 tablespoons Dijon mustard
Salt and black pepper to taste

Slice Smoked Chicken into thin strips. Cover; set aside in refrigerator. Wash and drain spinach; remove ends and chop into 2-inch pieces. Cover; set aside in refrigerator.

Combine cheese, oil, bacon, vinegar and mustard in screw-top jar. Seal and shake until well blended. Cover; set aside in refrigerator.

After all ingredients have chilled at least 30 minutes, combine chicken, spinach and dressing in large serving bowl; toss gently. Add salt and pepper; toss again. Serve immediately while still well chilled.

Makes 4 to 6 servings

chicken salad

1 package (4 ounces) sliced almonds
2 cups cubed cooked chicken
1 package (10 ounces) frozen peas, thawed
¾ cup sliced celery
1 tablespoon minced onion
2 teaspoons lemon juice
¾ cup HIDDEN VALLEY® The Original Ranch® Salad Dressing

Toast almonds in 350°F oven until fragrant and lightly browned, 8 to 10 minutes; cool. In large bowl, combine almonds, chicken, peas, celery and onion. Sprinkle with lemon juice. Add salad dressing and toss.

Makes 4 to 6 servings

chicken & mushrooms with pasta & roasted garlic sauce

1 teaspoon olive oil
4 boneless skinless chicken breasts
1 jar (about 28 ounces) roasted garlic pasta sauce
1 cup sliced mushrooms
8 ounces corkscrew pasta, cooked and drained
    Grated fresh Parmesan cheese (optional)

1. Heat oil in large skillet over medium heat. Lightly brown chicken. Remove from skillet; cut into thin strips. Return to skillet.

2. Stir in pasta sauce and mushrooms. Cover; simmer 10 minutes or until chicken is cooked through. Stir in pasta. Sprinkle with Parmesan cheese. *Makes 4 servings*

chicken & broccoli with garlic sauce

1 tablespoon BERTOLLI® Olive Oil
4 boneless, skinless chicken breast halves (about 1¼ pounds)
1 package (10 ounces) frozen broccoli florets, thawed
1 envelope LIPTON® RECIPE SECRETS® Savory Herb with Garlic Soup Mix
¾ cup water
1 teaspoon soy sauce

1. In 12-inch nonstick skillet, heat oil over medium-high heat and brown chicken. Remove chicken and set aside.

2. In same skillet, add broccoli and soup mix blended with water and soy sauce. Bring to a boil over high heat.

3. Return chicken to skillet. Reduce heat to low and simmer covered 10 minutes or until chicken is thoroughly cooked. Serve, if desired, over hot cooked rice. *Makes 4 servings*

chicken & mushrooms with pasta & roasted garlic sauce

ginger plum chicken

2 tablespoons peanut oil

8 ounces chicken (boneless breast or thigh), cut into 1-inch pieces

3 tablespoons LEE KUM KEE® Premium Brand or Panda Brand or Choy Sun Oyster Sauce

1 tablespoon thinly sliced fresh ginger

½ red bell pepper, cut into 1-inch pieces

½ green bell pepper, cut into 1-inch pieces

1 carrot, cut into 1-inch strips

3 tablespoons LEE KUM KEE® Plum Sauce

1 green onion, chopped

Hot cooked noodles

1. Heat oil in wok or skillet until hot. Add chicken, LEE KUM KEE Oyster Sauce and ginger; cook until chicken is almost done.

2. Add bell peppers and carrots; stir-fry 1 to 2 minutes. Add LEE KUM KEE Plum Sauce and chopped green onion. Stir-fry until chicken is cooked through. Serve over noodles.   *Makes 2 servings*

Prep Time: 20 minutes
Cook Time: 10 to 12 minutes

tip | Cut ingredients for stir-frying into the same size pieces for quick even cooking. To save preparation time, purchase precut vegetables for stir-frying. However, be prepared to pay more for this convenience.

ginger plum chicken

coq au vin & pasta

4 large or 8 small chicken thighs (2 to 2½ pounds), trimmed of excess fat
2 teaspoons rotisserie or herb chicken seasoning*
1 tablespoon margarine or butter
3 cups (8 ounces) halved or quartered mushrooms
1 medium onion, coarsely chopped
½ cup dry white wine or vermouth
1 (4.9-ounce) package PASTA RONI® Homestyle Chicken Flavor
½ cup sliced green onions

*1 teaspoon paprika and 1 teaspoon garlic salt can be substituted.

1. Sprinkle meaty side of chicken with rotisserie seasoning. In large skillet over medium-high heat, melt margarine. Add chicken, seasoned-side down; cook 3 minutes. Reduce heat to medium-low; turn chicken over.

2. Add mushrooms, onion and wine. Cover; simmer 15 to 18 minutes or until chicken is no longer pink inside. Remove chicken from skillet; set aside.

3. In same skillet, bring 1 cup water to a boil. Stir in pasta, green onions and Special Seasonings. Place chicken over pasta. Reduce heat to medium-low. Cover; gently boil 6 to 8 minutes or until pasta is tender. Let stand 3 to 5 minutes before serving.

Makes 4 servings

Prep Time: 10 minutes
Cook Time: 30 minutes

chicken marengo

⅓ cup olive oil

4 boneless skinless chicken breast halves (about 1¼ pounds)

12 ounces fresh, white mushrooms, sliced (about 5 cups)

2 cups frozen pearl onions, thawed

1 teaspoon minced garlic

½ teaspoon salt

½ teaspoon dried thyme, crushed

¼ teaspoon ground black pepper

1 can (14 ounces) diced tomatoes, undrained

½ cup dry white wine

Hot steamed rice (optional)

In Dutch oven, heat oil over high heat until hot. Add chicken; cook until brown on both sides, about 3 minutes each side, turning once. Remove chicken from pot. Add mushrooms, onions and garlic. Cook and stir until mushrooms are golden, about 10 minutes. Return chicken to skillet. Stir in salt, thyme and pepper. Add tomatoes with juice and wine; bring to a boil. Reduce heat to medium-low; cover and simmer until chicken is tender, about 10 minutes, stirring occasionally. Serve over steamed rice, if desired. *Makes 4 servings*

Favorite recipe from **Mushroom Council**

skillets *sans*

30-minute paella

    2 tablespoons olive oil
    1 package (about 10 ounces) chicken-flavored rice and vermicelli mix
    ¼ teaspoon red pepper flakes
  3½ cups water
    1 package (about 10 ounces) refrigerated fully cooked chicken breast strips, cut into pieces
    1 package (8 ounces) medium raw shrimp, peeled
    1 cup frozen peas
    ¼ cup diced roasted red pepper

1. Heat oil in large skillet over medium heat. Add rice mix and pepper flakes. Cook and stir 2 minutes or until vermicelli is golden.

2. Add water, chicken, shrimp, peas, roasted red pepper and seasoning packet. Bring to a boil. Reduce heat to low. Cover; cook 12 to 15 minutes or until rice is tender, stirring occasionally.   *Makes 6 servings*

sweet & sour stir-fry

    1 tablespoon vegetable oil
    ½ pound boneless chicken breast or beef, cut into thin strips
    1 bag (16 ounces) BIRDS EYE® frozen Sugar Snap Stir-Fry
    1 tablespoon water
    ½ cup prepared sweet and sour sauce

• Heat oil in large skillet or wok. Stir-fry chicken until cooked through.

• Add vegetables and water; cover and cook 5 to 7 minutes over medium-high heat.

• Stir in sweet and sour sauce; heat through.

• Serve hot over rice or pasta.   *Makes 3 to 4 servings*

Prep Time: 5 minutes
Cook Time: 12 to 15 minutes

30-minute paella

northwoods mushroom swiss melts

  4 boneless, skinless chicken breasts (about 1 pound)
3¾ cups water
  2 boxes UNCLE BEN'S® Long Grain & Wild Rice Original Recipe
  ½ cup chopped green bell pepper
  ½ cup chopped red bell pepper
  1 cup sliced mushrooms
  4 slices (1 ounce each) Swiss cheese

1. Spray large skillet with nonstick cooking spray. Add chicken, cook over medium-high heat 5 to 7 minutes or until lightly browned on both sides.

2. Add water, rice and contents of seasoning packets. Bring to a boil. Cover; reduce heat and simmer 20 minutes.

3. Stir in bell peppers; sprinkle mushrooms over chicken. Continue cooking, covered, 5 to 8 minutes or until chicken is no longer pink in center.

4. Place cheese over chicken. Remove from heat; let stand covered 5 minutes or until cheese is melted.

Makes 4 servings

cantonese chicken stir-fry

  2 to 3 tablespoons canola or peanut oil
  1 package (about 1 pound) PERDUE® Seasoned Boneless
     Chicken Breasts, Teriyaki, cut in thin strips
  3 to 4 scallions, washed and thinly sliced
  1 teaspoon minced fresh gingerroot (optional)
  1 package (about 1⅓ pounds) frozen Cantonese stir-fry mixture

In large, nonstick skillet or wok over medium-high heat, heat oil. Add chicken and stir-fry 4 to 5 minutes. Add scallions and ginger; stir-fry 1 minute. Add vegetable stir-fry mixture and follow package directions for cooking. Serve over oriental noodles or rice.

Makes 4 servings

chicken pomodoro with tomato basil garlic

  4 teaspoons olive oil
  8 boneless skinless chicken breast halves
  8 ounces fresh mushrooms, sliced
  2 cans (14¼ ounces each) Italian-style stewed tomatoes
  8 teaspoons MRS. DASH® Tomato Basil Garlic Seasoning
  ½ cup semi-dry white wine (optional)

Heat oil in nonstick skillet. Add chicken and brown over medium heat about 10 minutes, turning once. Add remaining ingredients. Bring to a boil; reduce heat and simmer, uncovered, 15 minutes.   *Makes 8 servings*

honey-glazed chicken

  1 can (20 ounces) pineapple chunks in juice
  1 tablespoon cornstarch
  2 tablespoons honey
  1 tablespoon Dijon mustard
  ½ teaspoon ground ginger
  ¼ teaspoon red pepper flakes
  1 tablespoon oil
  1 pound boneless skinless chicken breasts, cut into 2-inch pieces
  1 green or red bell pepper, cut into chunks
    Hot cooked rice (optional)

1. Drain and reserve pineapple. Combine pineapple juice and cornstarch in small bowl; stir until smooth. Add honey, mustard, ginger and red pepper flakes; mix well.

2. Heat oil in large skillet over medium-high heat. Add chicken; cook and stir 5 minutes or until browned. Add bell pepper; cook and stir 3 minutes. Add reserved pineapple and juice mixture. Bring to a boil. Reduce heat to medium-low. Simmer 5 to 8 minutes or until chicken is cooked through and sauce thickens. Serve with rice.

Makes 4 servings

chicken with tomato-basil cream sauce

4 boneless, skinless chicken breast halves (about 1¼ pounds), pounded, if desired
3 tablespoons I CAN'T BELIEVE IT'S NOT BUTTER!® Spread, divided
2 plum tomatoes, chopped
1 small onion, chopped
¼ teaspoon salt
¼ cup dry white wine or chicken broth
½ cup whipping or heavy cream
2 tablespoons loosely packed fresh basil leaves, cut in thin strips

Season chicken, if desired, with salt and ground black pepper.

In 12-inch nonstick skillet, melt 2 tablespoons I Can't Believe It's Not Butter!® Spread over medium-high heat and cook chicken 8 minutes or until chicken is thoroughly cooked, turning once. Remove chicken and set aside.

In same skillet, melt remaining 1 tablespoon I Can't Believe It's Not Butter!® Spread and cook tomatoes, onion and salt, stirring occasionally, 3 minutes or until tomatoes are tender. Stir in wine and cook, stirring occasionally, 2 minutes or until wine evaporates. Stir in cream. Reduce heat to low and return chicken to skillet. Simmer uncovered 4 minutes or until sauce is thickened and chicken is heated through. Garnish with basil.

Makes 4 servings

asian noodles with vegetables and chicken

1 tablespoon vegetable oil

2 cups sliced shiitake or button mushrooms

2 cups fresh snow peas, sliced diagonally in half

2 packages (1.6 ounces each) garlic and vegetable instant rice noodle soup mix

2 cups boiling water

2 packages (about 6 ounces each) refrigerated fully cooked chicken breast strips, cut into pieces

¼ teaspoon red pepper flakes

2 tablespoons fresh lime juice

1 tablespoon soy sauce

2 tablespoons chopped cilantro or sliced green onion

1. Heat oil in large skillet over medium-high heat. Add mushrooms and snow peas; cook 2 to 3 minutes or until peas are crisp-tender. Remove from skillet; set aside.

2. Break up noodles in soup mix. Add noodles, 1 seasoning packet, water, chicken and red pepper flakes to skillet; mix well. Cook over medium-high heat 5 to 7 minutes or until liquid thickens. Stir in reserved vegetables, lime juice and soy sauce. Sprinkle with cilantro. Serve immediately. *Makes 4 servings*

tip | Ramen noodles or noodles from instant soup mixes cook much more quickly than rice and pasta. Keep a supply on hand for a variety of simple meal solutions. Break up dry noodles to use in place of croutons in salads. Serve cooked noodles instead of rice with stir-fries. Or, use cooked noodles as the foundation for a Thai-style salad made with noodles, chicken and peanuts.

snappy skillets

asian noodles with
vegetables and chicken

chicken florentine in minutes

　　3 cups water

　　1 cup milk

　　2 tablespoons butter

　　2 packages (about 4 ounces each) fettuccine Alfredo or stroganoff pasta mix

　　4 cups fresh baby spinach, coarsely chopped

　　¼ teaspoon black pepper

　　1 package (about 10 ounces) refrigerated fully cooked chicken breast strips, cut into bite-size pieces

　　¼ cup diced roasted red peppers

　　¼ cup sour cream

1. Bring water, milk and butter to a boil in large saucepan over medium-high heat. Stir in pasta mixes, spinach and black pepper. Reduce heat to medium. Cook 8 minutes or until pasta is tender, stirring occasionally.

2. Stir in chicken and red peppers. Cook 2 minutes or until hot. Remove from heat. Stir in sour cream.

Makes 4 servings

simple stir-fry

　　1 tablespoon vegetable oil

　12 boneless, skinless chicken breast tenderloins, cut into 1-inch pieces

　　1 bag (1 pound) frozen stir-fry vegetable mix

　　2 tablespoons soy sauce

　　2 tablespoons honey

　　2 (2-cup) bags UNCLE BEN'S® Boil-in-Bag Rice

1. Heat oil in large skillet or wok. Add chicken; cook over medium-high heat 6 to 8 minutes or until lightly browned. Add vegetables, soy sauce and honey. Cover and cook 5 to 8 minutes or until chicken is no longer pink in center and vegetables are crisp-tender.

2. Meanwhile, cook rice according to package directions. Serve stir-fry over rice.　　*Makes 4 servings*

chicken florentine in minutes

chicken and linguine in creamy tomato sauce

1 tablespoon olive oil
1 pound boneless, skinless chicken breasts, cut into ½-inch strips
1 jar (1 pound 10 ounces) RAGÚ® Old World Style® Pasta Sauce
2 cups water
8 ounces linguine or spaghetti
½ cup whipping or heavy cream
1 tablespoon chopped fresh basil leaves *or* ½ teaspoon dried basil leaves, crushed

1. In 12-inch skillet, heat olive oil over medium heat and brown chicken. Remove chicken and set aside.

2. In same skillet, stir in Ragú Pasta Sauce and water. Bring to a boil over high heat. Stir in uncooked linguine and return to a boil. Reduce heat to low and simmer covered, stirring occasionally, 15 minutes or until linguine is tender.

3. Stir in cream and basil. Return chicken to skillet and cook 5 minutes or until chicken is thoroughly cooked.

Makes 4 servings

Prep Time: 10 minutes
Cook Time: 30 minutes

creamy chicken & broccoli alfredo

6 ounces uncooked fettuccini pasta
1½ cups fresh or frozen broccoli florets
1 small onion, sliced; slices cut in half
2 tablespoons butter or margarine
1 (10-ounce) can HORMEL® chunk breast of chicken, drained and flaked
1 (10-ounce) container refrigerated alfredo sauce

Cook pasta according to package directions. In large skillet, sauté broccoli and onion in butter until broccoli is crisp tender. Stir in chunk chicken and alfredo sauce. Cook, stirring constantly, until sauce is thoroughly heated. Serve over hot cooked pasta.

Makes 6 servings

chicken and linguine in
creamy tomato sauce

skillet chicken, mushrooms and vegetables

3 tablespoons bottled Italian dressing, divided
1 pound boneless skinless chicken breasts
1 pound fresh white mushrooms, sliced
2 plum tomatoes, diced
1 large carrot, cut in matchsticks or thinly sliced*
3 green onions, sliced
  Steamed rice (optional)

*For carrot matchsticks, cut carrot into thin diagonal slices; stack 3 or 4 slices and cut in narrow sticks.

Heat 1 tablespoon dressing in large nonstick skillet over medium-high heat. Add chicken; cook about 2 minutes or until browned. Remove and set aside. Add remaining 2 tablespoons dressing to same skillet. Add mushrooms; cook 4 minutes stirring frequently, until mushrooms begin to release their liquid. Stir in tomatoes, carrot and reserved chicken. Reduce heat; cover and simmer 10 minutes or until juices run clear when chicken is pierced with fork. Remove chicken and vegetables to heated platter. Cook sauce in skillet 2 minutes to thicken slightly; pour over chicken. Sprinkle with green onions. Serve with steamed rice, if desired.

Makes 4 servings

Prep and Cook Time: about 25 minutes

Favorite recipe from **Mushroom Council**

quick chicken jambalaya

    8 boneless, skinless chicken thighs, cut into bite-size pieces
  ¼ teaspoon garlic salt
    1 tablespoon vegetable oil
2½ cups 8-vegetable juice
    1 bag (16 ounces) frozen pepper stir-fry mix
  ½ cup diced cooked ham
    1 teaspoon hot pepper sauce
1¾ cups quick cooking rice, uncooked

Sprinkle garlic salt over chicken. In large nonstick skillet, place oil and heat to medium-high temperature. Add chicken and cook, stirring occasionally, 8 minutes or until chicken is lightly browned. Add vegetable juice, pepper stir-fry mix, ham and hot pepper sauce. Heat to boiling; cover and cook over medium heat 4 minutes. Stir in rice; heat to boiling. Cover, remove pan from heat and let stand 5 minutes or until rice and vegetables are tender and liquid is absorbed. *Makes 4 servings*

Favorite recipe from **Delmarva Poultry Industry, Inc.**

spanish skillet supper

1 tablespoon vegetable oil
1 pound boneless skinless chicken breasts, cut into 1-inch cubes
2 cups hot water
1 package (4.4 ounces) Spanish rice and sauce mix
2 cups BIRDS EYE® frozen Green Peas
  Crushed red pepper flakes

● Heat oil in large skillet over medium-high heat. Add chicken; cook and stir about 5 minutes or until lightly browned. Add hot water, rice and sauce mix; bring to boil. Reduce heat to medium-low; simmer, uncovered, 5 minutes. Stir in green peas; increase heat to medium-high. Cover and cook 5 minutes or until peas and rice are tender. Sprinkle with red pepper flakes. *Makes about 4 servings*

quick chicken jambalaya

chicken seville

 4 boneless, skinless chicken breast halves (1 to 1½ pounds)
 ½ teaspoon paprika
 2 tablespoons margarine or butter, divided
 1 (4.9-ounce) package RICE-A-RONI® Chicken & Broccoli Flavor
 1 cup orange juice
 1 cup sliced carrots
 6 large whole cloves garlic, peeled
 ¼ cup slivered almonds, toasted

1. Sprinkle chicken with paprika; set aside. In large skillet over medium-high heat, melt 1 tablespoon margarine. Sauté chicken 2 minutes on each side. Remove from skillet; set aside.

2. In same skillet over medium heat, sauté rice-vermicelli mix with remaining 1 tablespoon margarine until vermicelli is golden brown.

3. Slowly stir in 1 cup water, orange juice, carrots, garlic and Special Seasonings; bring to a boil. Place chicken over rice. Reduce heat to low. Cover; simmer 18 to 20 minutes or until rice is tender and chicken is no longer pink inside. Let stand 3 minutes before serving. Sprinkle with almonds.   *Makes 4 servings*

noodly chicken & green bean skillet

 3 tablespoons margarine or butter, divided
 ¾ pound boneless, skinless chicken breasts, cut into ¾-inch pieces
 1 (2.8-ounce) can French fried real onions (about 2 cups), divided
 ¾ cup milk
 1 (4.7-ounce) package PASTA RONI® Fettuccine Alfredo
 1 (14½-ounce) can French-style green beans, drained

1. In large skillet over medium-high heat, melt 1 tablespoon margarine. Add chicken; sauté 5 minutes or until chicken is no longer pink inside. Stir in 1½ cups fried onions. Remove from skillet; set aside.

2. In same skillet, bring 1¼ cups water, milk, remaining 2 tablespoons margarine, pasta and Special Seasonings to a boil. Reduce heat to low. Gently boil uncovered, 4 minutes, stirring occasionally.

3. Stir in chicken mixture and green beans; simmer 1 to 2 minutes or until pasta is tender, stirring frequently. Top with remaining fried onions.   *Makes 4 servings*